chibi Vampire
The Novel
1

STORY BY TOHRU KAI
ART BY YUNA KAGESAKI

HAMBURG // LONDON // LOS ANGELES // TOKYO

Chibi Vampire The Novel 1

Written by Tohru Kai
Art by Yuna Kagesaki

Translation - Andrew Cunningham
English Adaptation - Ian McDowell
Copy Editor - Peter Ahlstrom
Design and Layout - Jennifer Carbajal
Cover Design - Fawn Lau
Editor - Kara Stambach

Senior Editor - Nicole Monastirsky
Pre-Production Supervisor - Erika Terriquez
Digital Imaging Manager - Chris Buford
Art Director - Anne Marie Horne
Production Manager - Elisabeth Brizzi
Managing Editor - Vy Nguyen
Editor-in-Chief - Rob Tokar
VP of Production - Ron Klamert
Publisher - Mike Kiley
President and C.O.O. - John Parker
C.E.O. and Chief Creative Officer - Stuart Levy

A **TOKYOPOP** Novel

TOKYOPOP Inc.
5900 Wilshire Blvd. Suite 2000
Los Angeles, CA 90036

E-mail: info@TOKYOPOP.com
Come visit us online at www.TOKYOPOP.com

ISBN: 978-1-59816-922-5

First TOKYOPOP printing: January 2007
10 9 8 7 6 5 4 3 2 1
Printed in the USA

CONTENTS

"I'M SORRY...
IT'S HERE!"
A MOMENT
LATER,
HER FANGS
SANK INTO
THE BOY'S
THROAT!

"NO! SOMEBODY HELP!"

THE MAN GRABBED HER FROM BEHIND, PUSHING A HANDKERCHIEF AGAINST HER FACE.

RANKLED BY YOUICHIRO'S ICY TONE, KARIN TURNED AROUND. THERE STOOD KENTA, RED-FACED AND PANTING. HE'D FOLLOWED HER.

 **PROLOGUE**

As the sun sank behind the row of scattered houses, the sky turned rusty brown, like the color of dried blood. Karin Maaka panted like a basset hound as she ran through the gathering shadows of the nature park. The night wind kissed her feverish cheeks. *Quickly*, she thought, *I have to find someone now!*

Karin looked like a typical high school girl with her sailor uniform, satchel, and her unpermed haircut in a shaggy, layered bob. Her eyes round and white in her flushed face, she glanced around desperately. She ran deeper into the park, looking for all the world like she was fleeing from a pervert. Yet no cries for help issued from her parted lips.

There's someone!

Running faster now, Karin focused on a bend in the path where a boy sat alone on a pale granite bench. He appeared to be a high school student, but she didn't recognize his uniform. *Must be from a private school.* His features might have been pleasing, but his face was currently twisted in irritation as he glared down at the cell phone in his hand.

BA-DUMP, BA-DUMP, BA-DUMP! Karin's heart pounded.

Blood surged through every inch of her body, boiling over, roaring in her head like a rushing river. *Oh no, I can't hold it off any longer! I'm gonna blow!*

Karin was now deep in the miniature forest of the Shiihaba Nature Park, the twisting trees thick around her. Their gnarled trunks and branches hid people from view even during the day, so most visitors rarely followed this particular path to its end.

There was no one there but the boy. He was her last chance.

Hearing footsteps approaching, he turned warily toward Karin. He stood up as she closed the distance between them. And that's when she tripped. Not over some thick, treacherous root, but a pebble. A mere pebble!

Oh, no—not again!

She started to curse her chronic clumsiness, but the rising ground cut her off. Her face smacked into it with a jarring thump, rattling her blood-flushed brain. Everything went black except for sparking, red bursts of light.

"Are you okay?"

A strong hand wrapped around Karin's arm and helped her up. The boy's pale face swam into focus like the moon emerging from a cloud. He knelt before her, looking right into her eyes. Her headlong dash and subsequent tumble clearly had him worried.

"What's wrong? Were you running from something or to somewhere?" he asked.

At another time, she might have fumbled for some plausible explanation, but right now all she could manage was a reflexive moan. Her heart pounded so loudly—*surely he must be able to hear it.* Her blood was so hot that her veins felt like they were melting.

She'd heard about spontaneous human combustion; this had to be it. Not that the true cause of her condition was any more reassuring. The pain brought tears, blurring an already darkening world.

"Are you okay? You're burning up! Should I call an ambulance?" He fumbled with his cell phone; even in the dim light, she could tell he was flustered.

Wishing the sky would suddenly pour down cool rain, Karin wrapped her arms around his neck, hugging him tightly.

"Um, miss, you're choking me . . ."

"I'm sorry, but I can't stand it any more!" Karin's grip tightened around him.

The boy grunted in surprise at her strength. He couldn't see the canines emerging from between her slightly parted lips. Their size was comparable to those of a leopard; they were as sharp as the fangs of a cobra—and they were just as hollow.

"I can't ssshtand it any more!" Karen cried, her emerging fangs making her lisp.

"Um, miss, do you have me confused with someone else?" Held tightly in her grip, the boy suddenly knew why they called the transition from sunset to night the Magic Hour.

And then Karin sank her fangs into his neck.

The boy's body shook spastically. His eyes widened in shock. The light faded from them; the sky reflected such darkness. Karen held him tight, pressing her body against his, her fangs still buried in his throat, which in her feverish state felt as soft and cool as an ice cream sandwich. The wind carried the coppery whiff of blood.

At last her lips left his flesh. She took a tissue from her satchel and wiped her mouth as her fangs slid back into her gums. When the boy crumpled to the ground, she didn't even notice. He wasn't dead, just unconscious.

Karin was still panting. She wrapped her arms around herself and shuffled her feet from side to side in a clumsy little dance, unable to stop shaking in the afterglow, trying to hold in the blissful feeling that roared through her.

Wings flapped overhead.

A bat fluttered down out of the night sky and landed on the boy's head. It folded itself like an umbrella across his face and looked up at her with glittering black eyes.

"Anju, you came!" Karin said.

The roaring in her ears finally faded. Karin shook the cobwebs out of her mind and looked around, feeling a tinge of relief when she finally spied her younger sister standing in the shadow of a tree.

Anju wore a long dress garnished with quite a few frills. The black silk material contrasted with the hair that cascaded over her shoulders and down her back in platinum waves. Her face had high cheekbones and looked elegant, with no trace of baby fat, despite her tender years. Even Karin had to admit that she was breathtakingly beautiful, the kind of girl at whose delicate little feet a whole nation of Lolita-lovers would prostrate themselves with joy. But there was nothing lovely or graceful about the voice that cackled back at Karin. "Hah! Karin, you're puking pathetic! How much longer 'til you learn to clean up your own messes, ya good-for-nothing cow?"

The little girl's lips never moved. The wooden puppet's mouth simply clacked open and shut in time with those harsh words.

Karin stamped her foot, stubbing her toe on a root. "Anju! I asked you to stop using that stupid ventriloquist's dummy! If you're going to insult me, at least do it with your own mouth."

Anju's pretty mouth curled in a sarcastic grin. The doll continued its clacking stream of vitriol. "Yo, fish-face, learn how to do something as simple as erase a single human's memory before mouthing off at your betters. There we were, working away on our beauty sleep, when we get woken up early to deal with your latest *craptastrophe*. Maybe you ought to show Anju a little more respect for covering your bony butt."

Sighing, Karin bowed her head. "Sorry. As always, thank you."

Anju's expression softened and her lips finally parted. "Well, at least you got through it safely this time." She glanced down at the boy sprawled on the ground. "Pretty! Never seen that uniform. Must be from some private school for rich kids. But he looks about your age. You know him?"

"No. I ran out of time, had to find somebody quickly, and he was alone."

Anju tapped her foot delicately against the same root on which Karin had stubbed her still-aching toe. "You know this is going to happen to you every month, right?

Why don't you pick somebody long before you reach the crisis point? C'mon, Sis, learn from experience!"

"Yeah, I guess you're right," mumbled Karin, flexing her sore toe and rubbing her sore face.

"Next time, don't just go with the flow. Make sure you've got a good victim already lined up, same way you make sure you have a tampon ready."

Anyone with merely human vision wouldn't have been able to see Karin turn beet-red, but the single human present was still unconscious. "Please don't say that word so loudly!"

The phone lying next to the boy rang. His body twitched.

"The pretty boy is about to wake up," said Anju in a theatrical whisper. "I've erased his memories, so no harm done if he sees you. What do you think?"

"Ew, no! It would be too embarrassing if he ever suspected. Let's run for it!"

Karin bolted off down the path, running more like a moose than a deer, despite her delicate frame.

Anju followed, shoulders sagging. "You know, Sis, most vampires would be less worried about embarrassment than getting caught!"

"B-b-but it *is* embarrassing!" stammered Karin. "I can't help how I feel!"

As might be easy to guess, the two sisters belonged to an ancient family of European vampires, their ancestors having emigrated from the Carpathian mountains over two hundred years ago. Karin, however, had a number of qualities that made her unique among the "children of the night." Far from being advantageous, these qualities made

some members of the family question whether or not she could truly be called a vampire at all. More than once she'd been referred to as the family's greatest shame, and not just when she was out of earshot.

She had no ability to manipulate the memories of humans. She was fine with sunlight and garlic. Her night vision was not particularly acute, leaving her more than a little bit afraid of the dark. And most importantly, she *never* drank human blood.

It was all so embarrassing!

"You can stop running now," said Anju. "At this point, it just looks strange. Besides, if you keep it up, you're just going to trip again."

But Karin had already taken another nosedive. As she picked herself up, a bat fluttered down in front of Anju.

The delicate little girl met its beady gaze for a moment, and then imperiously waved it away. The bat chased moths through the halo of the nearest the streetlamp before skittering off into the inky sky.

"It says the pretty boy left the park and got into a chauffeured Benz."

Karin rubbed her sore knee. "Wow! I guess I was right when I thought he looked rich. Must be nice not to have to work a part-time job after school." She heaved an envious sigh. Being the only member of her family who needed to use the lights meant being stuck with the bulk of the electric bill. Not that this kept her from stubbing her toes on the furniture.

"Whatever," muttered Anju. "There's a more worrying problem with that boy."

"What? I didn't h-h-hurt him, did I?"

Anju snorted. "You? Not likely! But the bat says that as he got up, he kept saying, 'I could *swear* that there was a girl here'!"

"Eek!" Karin panicked, waving her arms like she wanted to join the bat in flight. The boy's memories had clearly not been completely erased. "Oh no, Anju, what will we do?"

Anju shrugged. "Some people are harder to wipe than others. But it's all good. Sure, pretty boy 'could swear' there was a girl there before he passed out, but so what? What's important is that he has no memory of being bitten." She smiled calmly. "The bat listened to his conversation with the driver. Turns out his house is pretty far away and it was only a coincidence that he was in this part of town. As long as he doesn't have your face in front of him to jog his memory, he'll stop worrying about it soon enough. Everything should be cool."

Karin sighed with profound relief. "Oh, thank goodness. Maybe I can be an ordinary high school girl again, at least for the next month!"

"Yeah, and for the next thirty days maybe I won't have to come rushing to your rescue. Playing the cavalry gets kind of old."

"Sorry, Sis." But Karin found herself thinking about the boy. She'd probably never see him again. They moved in very different circles, so much so that they might as well be living in different cities or on different worlds. What little he remembered of tonight he'd soon forget. He'd certainly never know she was a vampire.

I'm safe, she thought. *My toe hurts and my head hurts, but I'm safe. He was very handsome . . . but I'm safe, and that's what matters.*

Until three months later, in July . . .

THE BLOOD INJECTOR IS FREQUENTLY EMBARRASSED

It was the kind of morning that stuck to the skin; the air was heavy from the previous night's rain. A bird croaked somewhere up in the sky. The clouds looked swollen and ready to burst at any moment. Water slithered like tadpoles down soggy leaves.

Karin hurried toward school, wondering if the wet season was ever going to end.

I sure hope Maki brought her notes! she thought.

Karin had skipped school for the last half of June, staying in her room the whole time. Not surprisingly, her grades had been disastrous. Final scores were yet to be announced, but she knew she'd be retaking several exams. Math had been an incalculable fiasco and her English answer sheet had been nearly blank. Her teachers had probably run out of red ink.

In order to avoid summer school, she'd have to play catch-up for the next few weeks and get satisfactory scores on the makeup tests. Fortunately, Maki Tokitou, whom she'd known since elementary school, had lent her the notes for all the classes she'd missed.

Maki suspects I skipped because of Kenta.

The thought of her classmate Kenta Usui made Karin's cheeks flush red with shame.

He must think I'm so strange! How could he help it, after what he saw?

Kenta had transferred into freshman class 1-D in May. Ever since then, Karin's blood had been building up pressure like steam in a kettle. That wasn't a metaphor. He *literally* had that effect on her vampiric metabolism.

But of course Karin was a defective vampire and did not drink blood. When she bit someone's throat, she injected the surplus blood her body had generated into that person's veins. Instead of a blood sucker, she was a blood donor.

Or better yet, a blood injector!

Karin's body produced that vital fluid at an uncontrollable rate, generating more than her circulatory system could contain. Once a month, she had to get it out of her body. The best method was to bite someone and inject the excess into his or her veins. If she didn't, blood would spurt from her nose in a crimson fountain, leaving her unconscious from temporary anemia.

Collapsing in a pool of her own blood was horribly embarrassing! Naturally, she hoped to keep her unusual condition a secret.

But Kenta Usui had seen it happen.

My blood always increases abruptly when he's around . . . There's never been anyone who's physically affected me like that before!

See, every vampire had a preferred flavor of blood. Karin's mother loved the blood of liars. Her brother was drawn to those who were highly stressed out. She'd never noticed it before, but even a backward vampire like Karin had a type.

She was drawn to unhappy people.

Karin was unable to resist those who were sad or miserable through no fault of their own. That put Kenta Usui right in the center of her strike zone.

But I don't even know why *he's unhappy . . .*

Whatever his problems, he never let them show. He wasn't exactly the class clown, but she'd never seen him looking mopey or acting all emo.

I can't just ask him "Why are you unhappy?" because I'd sound like I was in some freaky cult!

When someone as unhappy as Kenta got near her, she'd be overcome with the urge to bite him and inject her blood. Responding to the impulse, her body began producing what felt like gallons of the stuff. Karin was utterly unable to control this reaction.

I can't believe he saw that!

She hung her head. Just remembering her nostril hemorrhage made her unable to lift her eyes from the floor.

It's bad enough I have to expel my extra blood once a month, but the passing out from anemia is even worse. At least it used to be a secret. Now this darn boy knows all about it!

The shameful knowledge that she was in the same class as a boy who could wreak such havoc with her blood cycle was what had driven her to skip for two weeks straight. She'd simply lacked the confidence to behave normally at school. More than anything else, Karin wanted to seem normal.

Her parents had screamed at her for skipping. Now that she knew unhappiness was the cause of her surging blood, she continued to go to school again. If she could somehow help Kenta overcome his sadness, the storm building in her veins would cease. She could get her life back again.

But she had no idea *how* to make Kenta happy.

Kenta was tall for a Japanese boy. When Karin stood close, she had to crane her neck to meet his gaze. His jagged, brown hair framed a wild-eyed face that looked more than a little intimidating. But he was completely different on the inside.

And I kept screaming and running away the moment I laid eyes on him! I even slapped him! He has every right to hate me.

But he hadn't been angry. He had heard her whisper, "Please don't tell anyone!" just before she fainted from blood loss. Not only hadn't he told anyone; he'd cleaned up the mess and snuck her out of the school by carrying her on his back.

Boys' shoulders are so broad.

Karin's heart beat faster at the memory. Nobody in her family had ever carried her like that. Kenta's back had been big and muscular and warm. Riding on it, she had felt completely safe and had drifted off to sleep like a little kid.

Oh God! That's so embarrassing! As she walked, Karin buried her face in her hands.

What was that?

It felt like someone was watching her. Karin stopped in her tracks and looked around.

"Oh, there you are!"

An elderly lady with a small dog was coming toward her. She shot Karin a toothy smile. The old woman always took her dog for a walk at the same time that Karin went to school, so they were a familiar sight to each other.

Karin relaxed, assuming that this was what had caused her feeling of being watched.

"Good morning. Hi, Lulu!"

She greeted the Chihuahua straining against its leash. The dog ignored her, lunging toward and barking at the bushes to the side of the path.

"Lulu, no! You'll get your clothes all messy!" The woman pulled the Chihuahua back and turned to Karin. "Dearie, I haven't seen you for ages. How have you been?"

"I had a little summer cold and then a bunch of makeup tests, so I've been going to school early."

"Oh, you poor thing! Is it all better now . . . ? No! Make pee-pee on the grass, not on the sidewalk!" The last command was addressed, obviously, to Lulu.

"Yes, much better, I just have so much work to do."

The old woman nodded indulgently. "You'll do fine, a smart girl like you! Take care!"

"I will, thank you. Have a good day, ma'am. Bye-bye, Lulu."

Taking her leave, Karin walked onward. The old lady led her dog away in the opposite direction.

Once the Chihuahua's shrill barking faded in the distance, the bushes beside the path shook. An older man in a plain suit emerged from the shadow of a tree. With straight comb marks in his slicked-down, salt-and-pepper hair, he looked every bit the faithful servant. Despite the

July heat, he wore a pair of leather gloves, which clutched a handkerchief doused in chloroform.

"Can't do anything with that dog around," he said in a flat tone of voice while watching Karin walk away. "Better find a different high school girl."

"Here're the notes, Karin. They were heavy!"

"Oh, Maki, you're a lifesaver," said Karin, hugging her friend in the middle of homeroom.

"Hey, not so hard on the ribs!" Maki gently extricated herself from Karin's clumsy embrace. "Give them back during class, okay? Or when we have homework. The faster you can finish with them, the better—I might have to take makeup tests, too."

"Of course!" Despite her agreement, Karin inwardly blanched at the thought of how expensive it would be to photocopy all the pages. But it would take much too long to write them all out by hand. Two weeks of notes were quite a pile. After all, these were for every class.

Almost every class.

"No English?"

Maki's shoulders slumped. She shook her head, sending her ponytail swishing through the air. "You know I suck at English. I got nothing worth lending you. You'd better ask someone else."

Karin nodded. "That's okay, you've already helped more than I deserve." She scanned the classroom.

"Hey, Fuku!"

Fukumi Naitou entered the room and paused in the doorway. "Yes?"

"Can I borrow your English notes?"

Her classmate's eyes crinkled with laughter behind her thick glasses. "Wow, you've been out awhile, haven't you, Maaka? Got up from your sickbed just in time for tests." Fukumi called everyone, regardless of gender, by his or her family name. Yet there was no malice in her brusque manner. Most of the students regarded her as a kind of blunt big sister.

Fukumi shoved her glasses back up on her nose. "So how bad did you do on the exams?"

"Don't say that word," Karin practically wailed. "I couldn't answer *anything* on Math or English. If I don't do well on the makeup tests, it's summer school for sure!"

Fukumi gave her a sympathetic look, put her bag on her desk, and took out her notes.

"I'll hand them over after third period today. Just give 'em back to me before class the next day. Let's see—yellow highlights are key points, so you'd better memorize all of them. Blue lines for stuff I thought might be on the test. Most cases, I guessed right."

Hearing that, Maki jumped in. "Oh, Fuku, can I borrow those when Karin's done? Pretty, pretty please? I'll probably need to take a makeup on English as well!"

Since there was hardly anybody in the room yet, Karin and Maki sat down next to Fukumi and got her to tutor them a bit.

"So, this sentence's construction . . ." Adjusting her glasses again, Fukumi paused in mid-explanation. "Say, not to change the subject, but where do you live, Maaka?"

"The western district."

"Then you go through Shiihaba Park on your way here? Better watch out!"

Maki caught Fukumi's drift. "Oh, you mean the serial kidnappings!"

Fukumi nodded grimly. "Yesterday, one of the older girls of my volleyball team said they got her friend."

"Really? Yikes! I don't care if they do pay you, it's just creepy." Maki and Fukumi shared a shudder.

Karin looked at them blankly. "What are you talking about?"

"Oh, right! You weren't here, and then we were too busy talking about tests. Nobody told you."

"Told me what?"

Her friends looked at her gravely. "You should stop cutting through the park," said Fukumi in a low voice. "Rumor has it girls are getting snatched."

Karin turned that ominous word over in her head. "What do you mean, 'snatched'?"

"You know, kidnapped! Drugged and hauled away. Several different girls, apparently."

Eyes bulging, Karin pressed for details. Fukumi had a lot of them, having just learned of her teammate's friend's misfortune.

There had been a series of incidents where girls walking to school through the Shiihaba Nature Park had been kidnapped. The assailant's modus operandi was to sneak up behind his victim and clamp a chloroform-soaked cloth across her face. She would then wake up to find herself blindfolded in a strange room.

Through the blindfold, her eyes could detect bright lights. The room was comfortably air-conditioned. Those sensations, along with the feel of the cushioned bed or sofa the girl woke up on, suggested this wasn't an abandoned warehouse or dilapidated building. It seemed to be someone's home, and a pretty nice one at that.

Still weak and woozy from the drugs, the girl would find herself unable to remove her blindfold or get up from whatever she was lying on. But then she'd suddenly be hauled upright and embraced.

Whoever he was, the mysterious assailant seemed disappointed, because he'd quickly release his victim, dropping her limply back onto the bed or couch. There'd be the sudden stinging smell of more chloroform, then nothing.

The next thing each girl knew, she was waking up alone on an empty street.

"If it was just that," said Fukumi gravely, "it wouldn't be much worse than being pressed up against a stranger on a crowded train. But their clothes . . ." She lowered her voice. "Their clothes had clearly been taken off and then put back on. The hook on their bra was in the wrong place, or their stockings were twisted, stuff like that."

Karin's eyes got very big. "While they were asleep, somebody . . . had sex with them?"

Fukumi shrugged. "Maybe. Either that, or some pervert fondled them while they were unconscious. But isn't that bad enough? Anyway, there was a hundred thousand yen in each girl's bag. As if they could be bought off."

The price made Karin's brain start doing math.

How many months of electric bills would that much money pay? Not that it would be worth going through something so vile and disgusting, even if I wasn't awake to feel it!

Closing her eyes, Karin shook her head violently to clear it of such gross thoughts.

Maki pounded her fist on her desk. "That can't be settled by money. Maybe for girls turning tricks, but I'd be pissed!"

Fukumi frowned. "Yeah. At least one girl was so messed up about it she ended up breaking up with her boyfriend. The point is, Maaka, you'd better stay out of the park. At least seven or eight girls have been grabbed, maybe more. Some probably didn't tell anybody."

Part of Karin didn't want to believe something like that could happen, although another part of her knew full well that worse occurred all the time. "But if there's that many victims, why isn't it on the news? Didn't anyone call the cops?"

Fukumi stared owlishly over her glasses at Karin. "Would you? Imagine being barely able to remember anything because of the chloroform and whatever else he used, then having to answer a bunch of questions about it. The very idea tweaks me out."

Karin understood perfectly. None of the assaulted girls had called the cops, but they'd confided in their best friends. Of course the rumors began to spread.

Their notes utterly forgotten, the three girls leaned toward each other across their desks, talking in whispers now.

"I asked a friend of mine from junior high, but it seems like there aren't any rumors about this at other schools."

"Only ours, huh? And what's up with hugging them while they're still clothed?"

"That's the weird part. They say at least one girl heard his voice. 'Not her,' he said, sounding annoyed."

Fukumi grunted, then looked at the ceiling, "Maybe he's looking for somebody," she murmured. "Checking to see if it's her by hugging her."

As disturbing as this mystery was, it made Karin forget about her own issues. "There's gotta be a reason why he always grabs them at the nature park!"

Fukumi looked at her gravely. "Yeah, I've been wondering about that. Maybe he hugged a girl in this school's uniform in the park and is trying to find her again."

"Wow! You're like a detective!"

Fukumi puffed on her pencil as if it were a pipe. "Elementary, my dear Maki. If the constables would only consult me, the culprits would be apprehended by tea time." She laughed sardonically. "Whatever. Don't believe everything I blather about. The whole idea's ridiculous."

Maki grinned. "Yeah, if he'd gotten that close, why doesn't he remember her face?"

Fukumi laughed, but the best that Karin could manage was an awkward shrug. *Shiihaba Nature Park . . . Hugged by a girl from this school . . . Crap!*

She had a nasty hunch who that girl might be. So far, Anju had erased the memories of everyone Karin had bitten. But even with her little sister's help, it was difficult for Karin to attack people from her school or job. Complete strangers made much safer victims.

Sheltered from prying eyes by its tall, twisting trees, Shiihaba Nature Park was great for getting away from it all. Not the best place to play ball, toss a Frisbee, or fly a kite . . . but for a quiet walk in the woods or sitting lost in thought on a bench, it couldn't be beat. Which meant it was easy to find people hanging out alone there, with no pesky witnesses. It was as if the park had been made for Karin's purposes.

Could someone she attacked there have recovered a few vague memories? Was that person now searching for her? She didn't want to think so, but it now seemed disturbingly plausible.

The thought gave her goose bumps.

If the kidnapper is really after me, what the heck does he want to do when he finds me?

It couldn't be anything good. He had knocked the other girls out and done nasty things to them even though he knew they weren't the girl he'd been seeking. If the kidnapper was truly looking for Karin, he surely had something even worse in mind.

If he catches me, it'll be more than just a quick one while I'm unconscious. Ew!

As imagined fates raced through her mind, her brain began to overheat. *But I've never even held a boy's hand, much less kissed a guy . . . !*

Sure, once a month she'd wrap her arms around someone and bite them, but that was purely desperate instinct and done regardless of age or gender. A far cry from hugs and kisses. The closest contact she'd ever had with a boy was the piggyback ride Kenta Usui gave her after she'd passed out from anemia.

The Blood Injector Is Frequently Embarrassed

Oh God! If he kidnaps me, what'll he do when he finds out I'm a vampire? That would be so embarrassing!

Dizzy with shame and anxiety, she put her head in her hands, not caring if Fukumi or Maki noticed.

Somebody suddenly tapped her on the shoulder. "Hey, Maaka!"

Reflexively, Karin shrieked. The sudden scream killed all conversation in the room.

Coming to her senses, she peeked out from between her fingers. Fukumi and Maki were both staring at her in horror. Reluctantly, she turned to see who had tapped her shoulder.

Kenta Usui's eyes were open so wide his pupils were islands in twin seas of white. The hand that had touched her was frozen in midair.

"Eeeeeek! Kenta, I'm sorry!"

Karin leapt up, but tripped over her own chair and fell head over heels, her pleated skirt bunched up around her waist. Kenta yelped and took a step backward.

"Karin!" Maki rushed to help her up, but it was too late. Kenta had been given an eyeful already. His attempt at a poker face might have been more effective if it wasn't the bright red color of tuna *sashimi*.

Helped to her feet by Maki, Karin managed to get back in her seat and speak. "Good morning, Kenta . . ."

"Hi, Karin." Still red faced, he looked down at her, fumbling for words. "Um, my seat . . ."

"What?"

"That's my seat. May I sit down?"

"Aaaugh!"

Karin once again sprang up and once again fell over. Kenta had to dodge her tumble.

Maki buried her head in her hands, moaning. At least this time Karin didn't flash anybody.

What on earth is wrong with her?

Kenta Usui sighed. He was trying to pay attention to the class, but kept staring at the back of the strange girl two seats up and over.

Unaware of his gaze, Karin was desperately copying the entire contents of the blackboard. She was apparently having trouble keeping up after her long absence. Kenta didn't have to see her face to sense her misery.

She looked like any other high school girl, so why was he fascinated?

I just don't get it. Maaka.

Ever since he'd transferred, he'd been sort of tangled up with Karin. Sometimes literally.

It started on his first day. No sooner had he said hello to everyone, then she'd fallen over with anemia and needed to go to the nurse's office. The teacher had told him to sit in Karin's seat until lunch, when they would fetch one for him, but Karin had come back from the nurse's office faster than expected. He'd scrambled up to give the seat back to her, but she'd put her hand over her mouth like she was about to throw up, and ran out of the room.

Was she afraid of him? He knew he had an intimidating face, but he hated to think that just the sight of him could make someone run away.

Then that evening he had seen Karin in the park with her arms around a businessman.

He'd heard enough stories about big-city schoolgirls with slack morals supplementing their incomes that way, so he shouldn't have been shocked. Still, Karin didn't seem like the type. Not that he'd ever known that type personally, but Karin didn't have a new cell phone or an iPod. She wasn't carrying around a brand-name bag. She wore no makeup or accessories. It wasn't like she was living the high life.

Also, she was absurdly clumsy. She would fall over and flash her panties all the time. Once at their part-time job, she'd slipped on a ladder and planted her behind in his face when he'd tried to catch her. Almost every time they met, he ended up red faced and embarrassed. And so did she. Not exactly his idea of a corrupt high school girl.

So then why on earth had Karin hugged that businessman?

Then a few days ago, Kenta had seen Karin embracing his mother. Not even in the most perverted manga did schoolgirls corrupt people's *moms!* So what had *that* been about?

He had a feeling he'd just scratched the surface of this mystery.

Karin said she has too much blood. Never heard of a disease like that.

His thoughts drifted back to the day before she'd stopped coming to school. He'd tried, as discretely as possible, to suggest that she stop prostituting herself. If his assumption was mistaken, that could be why she'd been avoiding him at school. Sure, Kenta regretted possibly saying too much. But what could he do? She fled the moment they made eye contact, which made it pretty darn hard to apologize. He didn't think he'd said anything that justified this level of hatred. Her unjust treatment of him was starting to piss him off.

One time he decided that—come hell or high water—he was going to at least get a *reason* out of her. But when he approached her after school, she'd fled like a rabbit, and while she was less than graceful, the girl could *run*. Standing there with his mouth open, watching her bolt had been bad enough. But then Maki Tokitou had tugged and his sleeve and offered woefully inappropriate advice: "It's one thing to make a pass at Karin, but if you chase her too much, you'll blow it."

Apparently Maki had mistaken his look of annoyed frustration for ardent passion. He was beginning to feel like he couldn't catch a break.

Worse, there'd been a lot of witnesses to Maki's admonition. His face burning, Kenta had yelled, "You've got it all wrong!" Then he'd bolted in the opposite direction.

That crazy Maki! Why would she think I have a thing for Karin?

He just wanted to know why she was avoiding him.

But I never thought it would lead to what happened!

Kenta sighed, remembering the incident with all too vivid clarity . . .

He'd finally cornered her in an empty corridor. "Karin, please, just tell me why you keep running away!" Maybe not the smoothest approach, but he was getting desperate.

"Aieee!" Karin's small body had spasmed like she was being electrocuted. "Don't touch me!" she'd screamed. Then there was a sudden, sharp pain on the left side of his face.

He took a step back, stunned. She'd slapped him!

Karin was flushed such a vivid crimson that it made the beads of sweat on her forehead and the tears streaming from her eyes look like drops of blood. Recalling it now, Kenta wondered if that was a symptom of her condition. She'd certainly seemed miserable.

At the time, though, he'd not been so rational or forgiving. Instead, he was struggling to control the surge of anger he'd felt at being slapped for no apparent reason. He couldn't hit her back; she was a girl and he wasn't that kind of guy. For a moment, though, he really wanted to be that kind of guy.

"If you hate me that much then, fine!" he'd growled. "Go ahead and hate me, but have the decency to tell me *why!*"

She tried to dart around him, but he wasn't letting her off that easily. When she reached out to push him away, he caught her hand. "Give me a reason!" he practically shouted. "I don't even know why, and it's driving me crazy!"

The only answer he received was a geyser of blood in the face. Stepping back, he wiped his eyes, sputtering in shock. At first he'd thought she'd puked it on him, like somebody in a horror film. But no, it was a nosebleed.

Well, sort of. It was coming out of her nose all right, but not in a mere trickle. He'd seen a kid get his nose broken on the soccer field once, but even that hadn't spurted like this. It was coming out like arterial spray in a samurai movie, but with no special effects guys around to work a hidden high-pressure hose.

The floor around them was turning red.

"Hey, what's wrong with you?"

Instead of answering, Karin covered her face with her hands and fell to her knees. Her body shook; her eyes rolled back and streamed tears. Unnaturally long canines protruded from her mouth. He was going to run for some help when she finally spoke.

"My blood," she gasped. "It, well . . . increases. Every month, I make too much and have to get it out of me. If I don't, it overflows like this." Her nose was still bleeding, bright red liquid dripping onto her knees as she slumped over.

Kenta had never heard of any such condition, but that didn't matter. Whatever had made excess blood spill out of her nose, the result was so embarrassing it made her cry. And he'd been the one who chased her down until she couldn't hide it from him. He felt like such a rat.

"Please don't tell anyone," she whispered, her wet eyes fluttering closed.

And so he didn't. Instead, he cleaned up the blood and snuck the semiconscious girl out of the school on his back. They'd been lucky; nobody spotted them.

There's clearly something abnormal about her, he told himself. He'd never heard of a person's body producing too much blood, but how else could she bleed so much without suffering far worse than a temporary fainting spell?

"When you're around it makes me worse," she told him when she came to. "Please stay away."

But her condition is hardly my fault! Kenta thought. *It's not my fault she skipped school for two weeks straight either, dammit! But still . . .*

Why did he feel so guilty? Why was he so relieved when she got better and started coming to school again? Maki's words raced through his head again.

"You like her."

Yeah, right. Trying to stop the flood of unwelcome thoughts, he clapped his hands to his head.

A strange voice broke his reverie. "Gracious! Usui wants to answer so much he's raised *both* hands! Very good, Usui. Come to the front of the classroom and write the answers to the first three problems in the brackets."

"Huh?"

The teacher grinned at him and pointed meaningfully at the blackboard.

Crap! What has that girl done to me now?

The clock's pendulum swung to and fro, marking time with an ostentatious *clack-clack-clack*. It was an antique clock, its ponderously intricate gears the product of an era when nobody had been interested in making a timepiece run silently and preferred their hours proudly declaimed. But the room was large, the ceiling high, and the carpet thick, so the dampened sound was never irritating.

The room was luxuriously decorated with mahogany display cases and houseplants in ornate bowls. There was a king-sized bed with a wrought iron frame and black silk sheets. In the center of this luxurious space, a boy of about seventeen or eighteen sat in a leather armchair, looking like a prince on a throne. He seemed extremely annoyed.

In front of him, a middle-aged man in a dark suit bowed his head. "I was unable to capture one today. There were too many people walking their dogs or jogging through the park. And there aren't that many high school girls who walk alone."

"So you wasted half a day," said the boy, his displeasure obvious.

Despite his sour grimace, there was a refined beauty to his delicate features. Delicate, but forbidding. Especially when he was dissatisfied. Both his voice and demeanor accurately portrayed someone accustomed to being waited on. His good looks could be described as imperious or perhaps even haughty.

"So far you've brought me twelve girls. One dozen. All of them incorrect. Zero out of twelve is a lousy ratio, Sasaki. This method is inefficient. There's no telling how long it will take us to find the girl we're looking for!"

His servant nodded. "I understand, Master Youichiro, but it's not as if I had much to go on. All we know is that she attends Shiihaba High School."

The displeasure in the younger man's voice gave way to anger. "Don't you dare reproach me for forgetting what she looks like!"

"Heaven forbid," Sasaki said, hurriedly bowing his head.

Youichiro turned his back on the servant and contemplated the decorations.

On the side table against the wall was a vase filled with sandersonia and decorative asparagus. The pale orange, bell-shaped flowers stood out like glowing lanterns. They complemented the smoky green of the asparagus perfectly. It was a display to soothe the heart of anyone who looked at it.

Youichiro's expression softened. He turned back toward Sasaki. "I know I'm asking a lot. But there's nothing else I can do. No matter how hard I try, I just can't visualize her face. Remembering the uniform was the best I could do. But I'm certain she was there!"

Youichiro searched his hazy, three-month-old memories.

On the way home from visiting an acquaintance, the Benz's expensive engine had hiccupped, then sputtered to a halt. He could have summoned another car, but the nature park was nearby and the driver said it would be fixed in no time, so he had elected to take a stroll amid the calming greenery. There had been some recent unpleasantness in his life, and he welcomed the time alone.

The nature park was beautiful. It was like he was bathing in the forest.

But this feeling didn't last long. The sun set and bad memories swarmed in the pooling darkness. The driver seemed to be making little progress on the car, so he took out his phone in irritation, intending to call for a second one. And that's when his memories . . . stopped.

There was a girl, I'm sure of that much!

A girl who had embraced him. He had no idea of the context, of what preceded that touch. But his body retained the memory of her arms. Rather that embracing her back, his own arms had hung limply at his sides, so she must have been the one who instigated it. He couldn't remember if they did anything else just that she was there and then she wasn't. When he'd fully regained his senses, she'd vanished without a trace.

He couldn't remember who she was or why she'd been there, but he remembered *her*. The feel of her slender arms around his neck. The warmth of her breath. The clean smell of her body, without a hint of cosmetics, just the slight whiff of Floral Fresh from her shampoo. That silky hair had been somewhere between short and medium. It had brushed lightly against his neck and cheek.

The fragmented nature of his memories only made each individual impression more distinct. It couldn't have been a dream—his dreams were never so vivid and tactile.

"After she hugged me, good things began to happen, starting that very day. I made up with a classmate I'd been fighting with. We were able to attend the Arishima garden party as a family, all three of us. Even Father went, and he despises parties. That kind of thing never happens. The only explanation for it is that Fortune herself smiled on me."

"Or perhaps it's all just a coincidence," said Sasaki, as expressionless as a cat.

"I know that!" Youichiro stood up from the leather chair. Anxiety crinkled around his chocolate-colored eyes. "But I have to find her again! I've no other cards left to play! Unless you have a better suggestion?"

Sasaki's posture shifted from indifference to servility. He bowed his head and held his tongue.

Youichiro paced the room. Even the way the thick carpeting muffled sound of his footsteps grated on his nerves. Circumstances required that he recover that run of good fortune.

Lady Luck. It was all thanks to her. I have to find her. Find her, and get her to . . .

Managing to remember the design of her sailor uniform, he'd dispatched his butler Sasaki to investigate its origin. But being a student at Shiihaba High School just meant that she was only one fish in a medium-sized pond, a needle in a haystack. Remembering her face would have narrowed the search, but it was like her features were covered in mist.

But Youichiro was sure he would know her if he hugged her.

"We can't keep dragging our heels!"

Sasaki shook his head. "I know how you feel," he said meekly. "But I believe this is the safest course of action. Shiihaba is a public school. The students are all very common. Many of them will be of a low disposition. If they were to learn that you were the heir to the Juumonji fortune, Lord only knows what lies they would tell in their greed. But this way we can bring them here one by one, with our identity remaining hidden."

Instead of answering, Youichiro walked to the window. The neatly trimmed lawn took on a somber hue under the cloudy sky. His brow furrowed, Youichiro tried to collect his thoughts.

When he first announced his intention to search for his Lady Luck, Sasaki had said exactly the same thing. At the time he thought his butler's cautious approach sounded good, but now it appeared he had been naive. They'd already wasted the better part of a month!

For the last week, he'd been skipping classes, just so he could verify the girls. He came home as soon as Sasaki had kidnapped them on the way to school. Like today, the butler often came back empty-handed. They'd only managed to check twelve girls, and none of them were *her*.

From the window he could hear the sound of a television. Youichiro frowned.

His uncle's room was in the building diagonally across from his, on the other side of the garden. The window was wide open, and sounds from that room carried easily across the flowerbeds. Not only the sound of the idiot box, but his uncle's dim-witted guffaws as he watched his moronic entertainment.

Youichiro bit his lip. His uncle appeared to have nothing better to do except go out and get drunk, or sit around the house in his underwear watching worthless television programs. Could such a clod truly be the younger brother of a man as great as Youichiro's esteemed father? It was unforgivable that this lout could barge into his mansion and do whatever he liked just because Youichiro was a minor and his uncle had declared himself his guardian.

How long does he think he can get away with it?

Spurred by that thought, Youichiro spun around. "Sasaki, you will arrange for my transfer to Shiihaba High School immediately!"

Sasaki gasped, eyes bulging. "Master Youichiro!"

Youichiro dismissed his servant's outburst. "I've wasted too much time with this foolish kidnapping! I shall enter that school and find her myself."

Sasaki stared at his master with codfish eyes, his mouth open in surprise. It was a moment before he was able to speak. "An heir to the Juumonji family going to a public school with the unwashed masses? Master Youichiro, think of what you're saying!"

Youichiro's smile suggested he found the idea amusing. "I'm not going to stay there 'til graduation. Just until I find her. Less than a month."

"It is not the duration I am concerned about; it's the blot on your transcript! Please leave this matter in my hands, Master Youichiro! You don't know the dangers of the world." Sasaki's fierce scowl seemed very out of place on his usually-expressionless face.

Despite his butler's out-of-character insistence, Youichiro stuck to his guns, irked by the accusations of naivety. "I know a bit more about high school than you do, Sasaki. All anyone cares about is where you graduate from. Once I've done that, I'm going to spend a year studying in England anyway; it's not like a one-month detour is going to matter. We can call it an experiment in social anthropology. I'll take over the Juumonji Group. It's hardly a bad thing for a leader to know how the common folk live—common folk will make up the bulk of my employees."

While his initial inspiration was to find the mysterious girl, he began to feel the persuasive weight of his own arguments. Youichiro had been attending the very best private institutions from preschool until now, his senior year of high school, and he'd been surrounded by the same faces the entire time. It had become damn boring.

"I'll start tomorrow. Or the day after, if I must take an admission test first, but I'll wait no longer than that. Make the arrangements for me to transfer to Shiihaba High School, Sasaki."

Sasaki started to say something else, but Youichiro cut him off with a wave of his hand. The discussion was over. It's not like there was danger of him failing the admission test, not with his grades. The only challenge would be how to find the girl in question. He could hardly go around hugging all the girls at the school; that would be too . . . common.

No, he would have to guess from general appearance, trust his instinctive reactions, and then find a way to confirm any promising hunches. It would be tricky, but certainly easier than kidnapping each of the hundreds of girls at the school individually.

I've no time for curiosity, no time at all. I'm going to find her!

For the second day in a row, the low-hanging clouds were gray with the promise of rain.

At the sound of the bell, the teacher made for the door like a horse out of the starting gate. Right on his heels were the hot-lunch students, dashing for the cafeteria and vending machines. About half the students remained in the classroom.

Maki stood up and brought her *bento* box over to the seat in front of Karin. "I don't know about you, but I'm starving."

Karin felt like sobbing into her own boxed lunch. "Makiiii! I didn't understand a *word* of that! I am so going to fail the makeup test!"

She'd already returned the notes Maki had given her, after painstakingly copying them, but it's not like there'd been any real time to actually read them.

Her friend patted her on the head. "Now, now, it's not as bad as that. Math is just a matter of building on what you learned before. Just go over those two weeks you missed and you'll be caught up. It should only take a few hours."

"That's easy for you to say," sighed Karin. "I have to work."

School was not the only place she'd avoided by pretending to be sick. She hadn't gone to her part-time job at Julian's, either. Scrambling to make up for lost wages, she'd been working extra shifts the past few days, which had left her barely any time to study.

Her friendly boss hadn't yelled at her, but simply asked if she felt better. But that only made it even harder to ask him for more time off to study. Besides, without the extra hours at work, she'd never be able to pay the electric bill.

"I'm doomed to summer school," groaned Karin forlornly, picking at her rice.

Maki peeked at Karin's meal, tilting her head to one side. "Your lunches are getting worse."

"I've got no time to make anything better. Especially now that I'm scared to cut through the park; it takes so much longer to get to school."

Maki shuddered. "Can't believe I'd forgotten about the kidnappings. Let's hope they catch the bastard soon."

The classroom doors flew open, catching Karin in mid-nod. She swiveled to see classmates Chiki Ootani and Asako Sada coming back from lunch, their faces flushed and eyes sparkling. The girls seemed both happy and excited.

Asako skipped toward them, arms flailing. "Maki! Karin! Wait 'til you hear . . ."

"You guys can't have finished eating yet," said Maki in surprise. "Did you forget your wallet or something?"

"Lunch? Who has time for lunch? You couldn't eat if you saw this guy either! He's incredible!"

"And so handsome!" trilled Chiki. "Like a prince in a fairy tale!"

Karin and Maki blinked in surprise. "Who?"

"The new third-year transfer student. Didn't you hear?"

"Asako and I just went to see him," sighed Chiki. "He's like a model! And it's not just his face! His family are former nobility, he got a perfect score on the admissions test, and he actually transferred here from Ginrei Academy! I mean, could he *be* any more perfect?"

Chiki's gushing had gotten progressively louder with each sentence. Not surprisingly, every girl in the class was listening intently.

"*The* Ginrei Academy?" squealed one. "The private school for rich kids?"

Asako and Chiki nodded in unison.

"Why would anyone transfer here from Ginrei? Did his family go bankrupt or something?"

Asako snorted. "If they had, he'd hardly be driven to school by his chauffeur, would he? Must be some sort of whim. Anyway, he's *hot*. Maybe a little snooty, maybe not the most approachable-looking boy you've ever seen, but it *works* for him. He's genuine high society. Name's Youichiro Juumonji."

Hearing that, one girl's head snapped round. "Juumonji! I've seen that name on the news. Haven't you heard of the Juumonji Group? Juumonji Chemicals, Juumonji Manufacturing, all kinds of big money stuff."

"Oh, so that's him," said another girl. "I heard the teachers talking—he's the only son of the head of the Juumonji Group!"

"You mean he's the company heir? No way!"

"Could be a meal ticket for somebody . . ."

The girls erupted in cacophony of squeals and whispers, while the boys began to grumble:

"Rich, good looking, *and* smart?"

"Sounds like something right out of a girl's manga. It can't be true."

"Don't sweat it. I bet he's a totally spoiled jerk. There's no way a society brat like that would be interested in our girls, if he even likes girls at all!"

But the girls didn't care about what the boys said.

"Where is he? I wanna see!"

"Third year, Class A. He was eating lunch."

"Let's go!"

Carried along with the excitement, everyone except Karin stood up.

Chika noticed that she still hadn't put her chopsticks down. "Don't tell me you aren't coming! How could you miss this?"

Karin flushed. "Ah, well, you know, it's just not my kind of thing."

Yikes, he's not a panda at the zoo, Karin thought. *It's creepy to go stare at him like he's some endangered species.*

Maki laughed airily. "Forget about her, Chika. Karin's already got Kenta."

Karin was flabbergasted. Seeing every other girl in the class nod knowingly, her flush deepened.

"Oooh, right, yeah."

"Have you seen how Kenta always looks at Maaka? You can tell he's serious!"

"Karin plays all nerdy and innocent, but she knows the game!"

"So how long have you two been a couple? Why didn't you tell us? We'd have thrown a party!"

"That's r-r-r-ridiculous," sputtered Karin. "Where are you getting this stuff? It's nuts." Her face was burning now. She could feel sweat dribbling down her neck.

Sure, Kenta is nice, but we're not exactly close! What's he gonna think when he hears these crazy rumors?

She looked around the classroom, relieved to see that Kenta wasn't there. *He must be in the cafeteria. Thank God.* If he'd witnessed this, she would have been much too embarrassed to meet his eyes.

"C'mon, Karin, there's no need to hide it!"

"Yeah, Maaka, we all know why you don't want to come gawk at the new guy. You don't want Usui to think you're cheating on him!"

"Or do you only have eyes for your boyfriend?"

If Karin had thought about it, she might have realized that her classmates were only teasing her because she'd turned redder than a sunburned beet. Unfortunately, her embarrassment prevented her from rationally analyzing the situation.

"There's nothing between me and Kenta and there never will be! Of course I'll come; I like cool guys just as much as the rest of you!"

And a few minutes later, Karin and the other girls were in front of class 3-A.

Class 1-D was not the only room that had been gossiping about him; the hall was crammed with girls jockeying for position like middle-aged women at the markdown tables. Yet they were surprisingly quiet and well behaved. Nobody shrieked. Nobody tired to force her way into the classroom. It was as if he exuded some sort of aura of delicious inapproachability that kept them from doing anything but peering in the doorway and whispering.

"Doesn't he look like that new model from last month's *Men's?*"

"No way! He's so much prettier. The boy is just dangerously hot. So my type!"

"But he's not exactly friendly, is he? Sure, he's good looking, but a little stuck-up."

"That's *why* he's so hot! A prince *should* be haughty."

Maki was over by the rear door, having successfully wormed her way though the crowd. She beckoned to Karin, "Over here!"

"Is it really worth this fuss? Just for a transfer student?"

Maki pulled on Karin's sleeve. "Oh, Karin, just be honest and admit you're too smitten with Kenta to even want to look at another boy!"

"I most certainly am not!" Caving under the pressure, Karin peered at the crack in the door.

In the last seat of the center row a boy was sitting alone, picking imperiously away at his lunch with a pair of ornate metal chopsticks. Clearly this was Youichiro Juumonji. It was a little hard to make out his face, but she saw him finish his meal and start packing the box away.

He was hardly being ignored. The other students in the room, especially the girls, looked like they wanted to speak to him. But it was as if they were all holding each other back—not that Youichiro's air of icy disdain made things any easier. He couldn't have been unaware of the people in the hall, but there was something about him that seemed to accept their curiosity as his due, even while holding them at arm's length. It was like he projected some sort of force field. Haughtiness carried to this level was a rare and magnificent thing.

Karin turned her head, trying to get both eyes lined up on Youichiro. And that's when it happened.

A powerful shudder ran from the base of her neck to the soles of her feet. Her heart revved like a motorcycle engine. And then came the blood, rushing through her veins with tremendous force.

Realizing what happening, Karin moaned. "Noooooooooo."

She wrapped her arms around herself and shook her head. She still hadn't gotten a good look at his face, but this was no time to fight the crowd for a better view. Forcing her rubbery legs into action, she squeezed backward though the cluster of girls around her.

The sensation was disconcertingly familiar.

It's just like when I'm near Kenta!

Her bloodsucker instincts—though in Karin's case, that was in blood injector instincts—had been triggered by some biochemical stimulus. She was sure her body was now producing blood at a terrible speed.

This can't be happening! I just got rid of it!

But her body disagreed. She wanted to bite him. She wanted to sink her teeth deep into his soft throat. To pierce his smooth skin and penetrate his throbbing jugular, to joyfully release all her excess blood into him. She wanted that blissful relief that made her feel like her whole body was melting. And she wanted it *right now.*

I can't! Not in school! Not in broad daylight!

Feeling her back hit the corridor's wall, she slumped to the floor. When Maki saw her go down, she forced her way out of the crowd and bent over Karin. "Are you okay? What's wrong?"

"I think . . . I think it's the anemia again."

Maki frowned. "But you're all red—shouldn't you be pale? Never mind, let's get you to the nurse's office." As Maki took Karin by the hand, there was a renewed commotion behind her.

The classroom door opened and Youichiro strode out, the crowd parting before him like the Red Sea before Moses.

Which left Karin directly in his line of sight. She was face to face with Youichiro, less than one meter between them.

Nooooooo! screamed Karin inside her head, immediately recognizing the boy she'd bitten three months ago in Shiihaba Park.

Oh God, why would he transfer to my school? Does he know what I am? Why is this happening to me?

His attention drawn by her limp posture, Youichiro stared down at her with his dark, imperious eyes. On his delicate face, hauteur gave away to puzzlement.

Feeling nauseated, Karin covered her mouth. Her breath rattled between her fingers and her blood pounded in her head.

Oh crap! This is really bad!

Panic giving her renewed strength, she sprang up like a jack-in-the-box, only to immediately trip and stumble to her knees.

Maki pulled her to her feet again. "Karin, what's wrong? Karin!"

Karin shook her off and lurched down the hallway. Each jerky step threatened to turn into another fall, but that didn't matter—she had to get away from him, and *fast*! It was as if her body were counting down to an explosion.

At the end of the hall was a staircase. She had to get down it and back to her classroom . . .

But of course she slipped.

"Aieeeeeeeeeeeeee!"

THUMP, THUMP, THUMP, THUMP! Squealing, she tumbled all the way down to the landing.

Maki was right behind her, well aware of her friend's chronic clumsiness. "Karin, are you okay?"

Several other students followed, their faces a mixture of concern and not entirely concealed amusement.

"Wow, you really took a fall that time!"

"Ouch, I felt that just watching it!"

"Yeah, that *really* looked like it hurt!

Maki glared at the gawkers. "Of course it did, you idiots! Asako, help me get her to the nurse's office."

Chagrined, Maki's classmates helped her gather Karin up and carry her down the stairs.

From the top landing, Youichiro watched, his proud head tilted to the side like a falcon's. There was something oddly familiar about what he'd just witnessed. There weren't many clumsy people in his familiar social circles.

The way she kept falling—I could swear I've seen someone fall like that before. What was the name I just heard?

Karin.

He rolled it around on his tongue, repeating it softly out loud. "Karin. Karin." This needed further investigation.

Karin was resting on a bed in the nurse's office, her eyes closed and a cool cloth on her head. She had fallen down twelve steps yet had nothing worse than a mild bump on her forehead. Maki had tried to convince her to leave school and see a doctor, but Karin knew she was okay. She'd been falling down all her life. There were judo black belts less experienced at it than she was. She didn't need a doctor; she just needed to lie still and nurse her aching head.

"I'll take fifth period notes for you," said Maki. "And I'll tell the teacher why you aren't there."

"Yeah, we got you covered. You just take it easy," said Asako with an expression that suggested she was feeling guilty for having just stood there and gawked at Karin's accident.

"Thanks," mumbled Karin, grateful but wishing they'd go away and leave her alone.

"And we won't tell Kenta that you went to see the transfer student."

"Shut up!" said Karin so loudly it made her head hurt more. "I told you he's nothing to me!"

"Now, now, getting upset's not good for a sore head! You just rest and think about your dreamboat! I'm sure he'll be in to check on you soon."

Everyone laughed, even Maki, until they saw how flushed with anger she was. Beating an abashed but still amused retreat, they closed the door after them. Karin flopped back down on the bed, sulking. She was all alone in the room, the nurse being off today for training at the hospital.

Kenta would be so mad if he heard what they're saying! Darn it, I've done nothing but cause trouble for that boy!

He wasn't her boyfriend; he wasn't her secret crush; he wasn't anything like what Maki and the others thought. But they were in the same class; they worked at the same restaurant; he had cleaned up after her spectacular nosebleed and then kept her bizarre condition a secret from everybody else.

Wow, she thought. *He really has done a lot for me.*

There was that time she fell off the ladder at work. He'd caught her. When she'd passed out, he'd carried her home. *His back—it felt so broad and warm and good.* Karin could feel herself blushing at the memory. She pulled the sheets up to her nose.

But he's just a classmate, nothing more! I can't help it if he stirs up my blood, but that's the only thing that makes him different from any other boys. Well, almost any other boys. That new third-year transfer student sure got it worked up too.

She fidgeted uncomfortably. *What was his name? Youichiro Juumonji. But that reaction isn't my biggest problem with him. I've bitten him before! He could identify me! Oh dear, what am I going to do?*

Smacked in the face by the seriousness of her situation, Karin sat bolt upright, knocking the cool cloth off her sore head. Picking it up, she pressed it back to her brow, trying to contain her thoughts.

It was three months since that fateful evening in Shiihaba Nature Park. What was it Anju had said, that her victims' memories weren't completely deleted? Her little sister had managed to erase the part about Karin biting him, but even that might not be permanent. Who knew what latent recollections might be triggered if Youichiro were to see her again?

God, this blood-producing vampire stuff is just too embarrassing! Why me? Why, why, whyyyyyyy?! Clapping her hands to her head like that famous painting entitled *The Scream*, she shrieked that last "why" aloud. The sound of her own voice shocked her back to her rattled senses.

She clapped her hand over her mouth, but the damage was already done. Or was it? Nobody came running. With luck, the hallway outside the clinic was empty and no one had heard her.

That was close! I've got to calm down.

She clasped her hands over her swiftly beating heart, ordering her rebellious body to control itself. If things kept going like this, she wouldn't need any mysterious transfer student to reveal her secret.

Does he even remember me? His face was so unreadable when I saw it in the hall—surely he would have looked more surprised if he recognized me. Man, I thought he looked like a rich boy that night in the park, but I would never have pegged him for nobility!

There was something else to consider. Her blood's reaction to Youichiro meant he must be unhappy. How could that be? If there was ever a boy who had everything . . .

It's certainly not lack of money. I can't imagine what it's like not to have to worry about that. Not that money brings happiness, but lack of it sure adds to stress. I don't even know how I'm going to pay for the darn electricity this month! But I can't think about that now.

Karin considered what could be making Youichiro so sad. Money was out, so what about his grades? That seemed unlikely; the tide of gossip sweeping through the school's female population carried with it the tidbit that he'd gotten a perfect score on his admissions test. Beautiful, rich, and smart—the boy was a bona fide triple threat.

Must be nice not to have to sweat exams! Argh, it's a good thing I'm not working today, since having to do that math homework is like having to pull my own teeth. And I didn't understand a thing that teacher said in class today. Why did I skip class for two whole weeks? That was crazy! I'm crazy. And now worrying about being recognized by the new transfer student is making me crazier.

What was I worried about? Oh yeah . . . What on earth can be making the boy so sad?

He was so good looking that on his first day of school all the girls were already treating him like some sort of rock star. All he had to do was ask, and just about any girl would take him. So she doubted he could be having problems in the relationship department.

I'm just average looking. I'm no brainiac. I'm pretty darn poor. And I'm not even a proper vampire—God, that was so dangerous back there. A few moments longer and I'd have exploded in front of everyone, showering them with blood. Then I really would've died!

Just the thought made her face hot. She covered it with the sheets.

Maybe because of the shock to her system from her hard fall down the stairs, the throbbing of her blood had subsided. But that didn't change the danger that Youichiro Juumonji posed to her. Between the way he stirred her blood and the possibility that he might regain his memories, he was a bigger threat than Kenta Usui.

Maybe he doesn't remember me, at least not yet, but I darn well better avoid him. Thank God we aren't in the same grade! At least I won't have to see him as often as I do Kenta.

The ringing bell signaled the end of fifth period.

Karin gingerly clambered out of bed. Her head still hurt a bit, but she was in a much better condition than she had been a half hour before. Along with her supernaturally fast recovery, the thought of falling even farther behind in class sent her back to her feet. This was no time to take a sick day.

Just as she got to classroom 1-D, the doors opened before her.

"Eeek!"

There was Kenta Usui, right in front of her. Not only did she squeak at the sight of him, but for a moment her arms beat the air like the vanes of a rubbery windmill. Miraculously, she managed to get ahold of herself and actually say something coherent.

"Um, hi Kenta. How are you doing?"

Kenta looked at her like she was from Mars. "How am I? Karin, you're the one who fell down a flight of stairs. At least that's what Maki said."

Great, her accident was already common knowledge.

Her face flared, and whatever words she'd been forming retreated back down her throat. Equally flustered, Kenta looked away. And so they stood there, face to face but not looking at each other, in the most awkward silence she'd ever experienced in her life.

It was Kenta who finally broke this Mexican standoff of embarrassment. His voice so soft that he sounded more like an elementary student than a high schooler, he stammered out a question while looking at his shoes. "Um, so, *are* you okay?"

She answered in the same flustered tone, the words getting a little easier as each one came out. "Um, yes. Fine. Just a bump."

"Good. That's good." A relieved smile softened his face.

Karin smiled back, then realized they were standing in the middle of the doorway, gawking at each other.

The same thing must have occurred to him. His naturally darker skin tone made his blush a maroon contrast to her hot pink. "Try n-n-not to fall down so much. You could get hurt!" Avoiding eye contact, he moved gingerly past her and hurriedly retreated down the hall.

Karin watched until he disappeared around the corner. Sighing for reasons she couldn't have explained even to herself, she went into the room. Thinking about the awkward but obvious concern in his voice, she felt something warm in her chest.

Or is my blood going off again?

Yes. Her cheeks were on fire again; her heart was revving up. This was bad.

Have to think about something else. How about Modern Lit? I only understood less than half of the homework. Maybe Maki could help me.

When she stopped thinking about Kenta Usui, the throbbing in her chest went away.

Thank God it wasn't the full-on blood rush.

Karin relaxed a little. Her heart was still beating a bit faster than usual, but she wasn't overheating.

This is all too much! The transfer student is making my blood rise, there's a scary kidnapper in Shiihaba Park—it feels like there's danger all around me. Maybe I should talk to mama and papa when I get home. But first, my biggest problem!

She hadn't finished her homework. Karin headed for Maki's desk.

 ## THE BLOOD INJECTOR
IS ACCUSED UNJUSTLY

The final bell of the day rang.

"That's enough for the day," said Mr. Shirai, their homeroom teacher. "Please be safe going home!"

Half the class dashed for the doors, but the others remained in their chairs a few minutes longer, gathering up books and chatting with friends.

"See you tomorrow," said Maki, squeezing Karin's shoulder. She had practice after school.

Karin smiled and nodded, stuffing books and papers into her bag. She had no extra curricular activities and wasn't on the schedule at work today. Unfortunately, this meant she needed to head straight home and catch up on her studying. Otherwise she was sure to fail her makeup tests.

I wonder if they caught the Shiihaba Park kidnapper. There aren't any new rumors, but that could just mean the victims have been too ashamed to tell anyone. I'd better not cut through it.

The crowded hallway was heavy with a strange, silent tension, but she didn't give it much thought, preoccupied as she was with the dangers that might lurk on her normal shortcut. She rounded the corner that led to the outer doors and stopped as suddenly as if she'd smacked into in invisible brick wall.

Youichiro was standing just in front of the doors. The superiority that he wore like a mantle drew all eyes to him and silenced all tongues.

Oh, God, why? Why him? Why me?

The fact that they were in different grades had allowed Karin to convince herself she would almost never cross his path. *Yeah, I sure called that one right.* It was as if someone had superglued the soles of her shoes to the linoleum floor.

Youichiro had been leaning against the wall, but when he saw Karin he stood up and looked her over with the cool indifference of a leopard at the zoo. Yet there was a hint of something else in those dark eyes. Was it a gleam of confirmation?

Stop it! she told herself. *You're just being paranoid!*

The hallway was full of students, with more leaning out the windows and doors of the nearest classrooms. He paid the gawkers no attention.

Please, stop looking at me like that! But she couldn't bring herself to say that or anything.

"Karin Maaka?"

Why did he know her name? Had he asked someone? Was his tone of voice deliberately rude, or just that of someone used to having all his questions answered? She had no time to consider these or any other questions. Still unable to speak, she jerked her head up and down like her little sister's annoying puppet.

Youichiro walked directly over to her, stopping only inches away.

Yikes, what's he doing?

An instant later, she knew. His delicate hands surprisingly strong on her shoulders, he pulled her into an embrace.

Their audience gasped.

His behavior was so unexpected she couldn't move, couldn't speak, couldn't scream. She was stiff as a store window mannequin, her thoughts an incoherent swirl of shock and embarrassment. And maybe something else.

Still gripping her tightly, Youichiro whispered in her burning ear. "I remembered. It *was* you who hugged me that day."

Karin made a strangled sound deep in her throat, then finally managed to form words. "You . . . remembered?"

Youichiro smiled with cold self-satisfaction. "And that confirms it."

She should have acted like she didn't know what he meant, accused him of being crazy, slapped him in outrage, anything but what she'd said.

I'm such an idiot!

Too late for a cover story. She had admitted it. It was all over. Youichiro was going to tell everyone in school that she was a vampire. Sure, he didn't know that she wasn't a *proper* vampire, that she injected blood rather than drinking it, but that was irrelevant.

Everything from her neck up grew very hot.

OhGodohGodohGod!

And that's when things got even worse. Her muscles spasmed, her heart thumped, and her internal temperature began to climb.

No! Not now, not here!

Her blood rush had subsided when she fell down the stairs, but some latent spark had remained. And now Youichiro had rekindled it. Karin was in big trouble.

She began to struggle.

"No! Get your hands off me!"

Looking puzzled, Youichiro loosened his grip . . .

"What the hell do you think you're doing?!" shouted a voice that mingled surprise and fury. "Let go of her!"

It was Kenta Usui. He grabbed Youichiro's arm and tried to pull it off Karin.

"Don't touch me," said Youichiro with cold disdain, shaking him off.

Taking advantage of this opening, Karin quickly backed away. Her legs were rubbery, but once she got her back against the wall, she was able to stay on her feet. Something white filled the field of her blurred vision.

It was Kenta's shirt. He'd thrown himself between her and Youichiro.

Kenta!

Karin's knees buckled and she almost collapsed. Every muscle in her body ached from clenching.

Not now!

She almost fell forward against Kenta's back, but managed to get one foot forward and stop herself. With her blood roaring like this, she had to keep her distance from him.

While Karin struggled with her own body, Kenta was unleashing a string of invectives at Youichiro. Even though the individual words weren't really registering, she could tell he was incredibly angry.

"What do you think you're doing? That's sexual harassment, scumbag. Couldn't you see Maaka was trying to get away?"

Youichiro raised a disdainful eyebrow. "Karin would hardly try to get away." He was already calling her by her first name!

"Who do you think you are? Get over yourself! She obviously isn't interested! Just because you're good looking doesn't mean every girl in the world wants you!"

A low murmur of assent ran through the boys in the onlooking crowd. Kenta might as well have been speaking for them.

Youichiro snorted. "I don't think anything of the sort. But Karin *does* like me. Why else would she have hugged me?"

Exclamations of surprise rippled through the crowd.

"No! Don't say that in front of everyone!" It was if a breaker had blown in Karin's head, the surging emotional shock shorting out not only her capacity for rational thought but her rising blood rush. Her body temperature spiked and sweat poured out of her like from a squeezed sponge.

Sputtering, desperately searching for words, she struggled to defend herself. "Th-that w-w-was . . . that was just . . ."

How could she tell him that there'd been no affection or desire in her embrace? It's not like she could say, "I'm a vampire, silly—I was just biting your throat!" Even if it were safe to reveal her family heritage, further explanation about how she didn't drink people's blood but injected her own into them was unthinkably embarrassing. Lost for a decent excuse, she simply buried her face in her hands, her body convulsing in panic.

Kenta turned around and stared at her, his face flushed purple. Over his shoulder, Youichiro continued to smirk. "Are you saying she's the kind of girl who would embrace a man she didn't like? That's not very nice of you."

"But I didn't—I mean, that was only . . . " she trailed off.

Karin couldn't decide what would be worse, him remembering being bitten and pumped full of blood, or this apparent misconception that she'd hugged him because she was in love with him.

Pushing past the rigid Kenta, Youichiro calmly continued to address the red-faced and tongue-tied Karin. "I transferred here to look for you. I need you. I'm so glad I found you." He waved airily at the crowd. "Forget about them. We hardly need to hide. Let the gossip hounds have their say. Why should we care?"

You may not, but I sure do!

There were now several layers of people surrounding her, Youichiro, and Kenta. She had to find a way out of this. But what could she say?

Oh God, please let me think of something!

Her eyes, blurry now from the onset of tears, tried to focus on Kenta's face. He was flushed and angry, his mouth curled in a grimace.

She remembered the time he'd seen her attack a napping businessman in the park. Unable to tell what she was really doing, Kenta had assumed she was turning tricks and later scolded her for her alleged immorality, saying, "I know you must have been desperate, but there have to be other ways to make money!" She'd never quite managed to explain her way out of that one.

Kenta must be horrified. First he thinks I might be a prostitute, even though a reluctant one. Now I look like some tramp who gropes total strangers. What am I going to do?

The thought was like a punch in the chest. She wanted to collapse and curl up into a little ball of agony. But then Kenta yelled something that distracted her from her downward spiral.

"Stop right there! That's no reason to assume Maaka likes you!"

It wasn't just what he said, but how he said it, with no trace of scorn or malice. If there was any outrage, it wasn't directed at her. Instead, he sounded confident and even protective, like he was trying to clear up a misunderstanding on behalf of a friend unable to speak for herself.

Is he . . . protecting me?

The sensation in her heart was a sharp one, but not like the awful throbbing pain she'd felt mere moments before. It was a shock, but a sweet one.

Grappling inwardly with this new sensation, she watched Kenta spin Youichiro back yelling directly in his face. "You think you're the only one she's hugged? Before she ever met you, I saw her with some businessman in the park! And then . . ."

The crowd wasn't just muttering now, it was practically roaring!

No, Kenta! What are you saying in front of everyone?

This time it was like a hydrogen bomb exploded in Karin's head, vaporizing all synapses. Anything would have been better than *this* defense.

Apparently not intending to elaborate, Kenta turned back to Karin, but too late. A running commentary was coming from the crowd.

"Karin hugged some old dude?"

"A businessman, yuck!"

"Why would she do that?"

"You know why! Why does any girl meet guys like that in the park or at the train station?"

"Does she need money that badly?"

Karin felt her schoolmates' stares like knives and their whispers like razors. Youichiro stared at her and Kenta in shock.

"That's not it!" she screamed. "That's not it at all! I can't take any more of this!" Outrage not only gave her the ability to speak but it broke her paralysis. Stiff-arming students out of her way like a male athlete twice her size, she charged down the hall, gaining speed with each clumsy but powerful step. Caught off guard by this unexpected retreat, Kenta and Youichiro could only stare after her.

"Interesting," said Youichiro with a nonchalance that might have been affected. He turned to face Kenta. "You're in this class. Name?"

Kenta was still looking past him at where the crowd had swallowed Karin. "Huh?"

"Your name is?"

Recovering slightly, he glared at Youichiro. "Kenta Usui. Who are you?"

Youichiro's face betrayed no emotion. "Youichiro Juumonji. If what you say is true, then Karin may not have any particular feelings for me after all."

Kenta's eyes widened at this blasé admission, but Youichiro wasn't finished yet.

"Ultimately, it doesn't matter. You appear to have a crush on Karin. Just as that's your business, what's between her and me is mine. I trust you will hold your tongue."

Kenta's ruddy flush spread to his collarbone. "Why should I?"

Youichiro's face was still a chiseled mask. "Am I wrong?"

"Don't try to confuse matters! I stuck up for Karin because I'm her classmate!"

Youichiro actually smiled at that, but without any added warmth. "That wild-eyed glare you're giving me suggests you have a more personal stake in this."

"My eyes are always like this!"

Youichiro nodded. "I beg your pardon, then. But if you're only her classmate, you won't need to interfere any longer, will you? Goodbye." With an indolent wave that Kenta could only take as mocking, he turned on his heel and walked away.

Kenta glared after him for several moments before becoming aware of the weight of the crowd's gaze. Flushing even more deeply, he strode in the opposite direction, not wishing to exit the school by the same route as Youichiro.

With all the actors gone, the audience began to disperse.

"That was *awesome*. Like a battle for love in a soap opera!"

"So what's up with Mister Hottie Transfer Student and that girl Maaka?"

"I dunno, but as long it makes for such an entertaining show, I hope they keep at it. Who do you think will win? My money's on Juumonji."

"Dude, no. I'll put a thousand yen on the freshman with the *Yakuza* glare. The girl looks like she's got a thing for him."

"Yeah, but when a guy's that good looking and that rich, he's holding all the aces. I think the Ice Prince is gonna nab her. Two thousand."

Where the boys had simply enjoyed the show, the girls had a different reaction.

"Karin's letting businessmen grope her for money? That's so gross, not to mention it gives the school a bad name."

"I don't think she's turning tricks; I think it's something else. That's what she seemed to be trying to say . . ."

"But why else would she have been embracing some middle-aged guy in the park? Even if he was her lover rather than just another customer, that's not exactly a good thing!"

"Yeah, and why would she hug and kiss Juumonji before she even knew who he was? Trying to get into his wallet by seducing him?"

"She's not hot enough to be acting like such a tramp! Who does she think she is?"

The girls' running commentary began to take on a hissing, catlike quality. Knowing better than to object, the boys held their peace.

Youichiro was surprised to see his butler Sasaki sitting behind the wheel of his Benz. "Why are you here instead of Nakaoka?" he asked, referring to his regular chauffeur.

"I was concerned for your safety."

Youichiro slid into the leather-upholstered back seat. The car hummed to life.

"How was your first day, sir? Were you assaulted by a violent teacher, threatened by a delinquent, or seduced by a high school girl with loose morals?"

Youichiro yawned. "Nothing so interesting as that. Everyone kept their distance. Most of the students never even spoke to me."

Sasaki clucked his tongue. "The so-called silent treatment is more subtle than the battery and theft I would have expected from such rabble, but it's still a form of bullying. We should never have allowed you to attend such a dangerous establishment. Please return to Ginrei Academy. I promise I'll find your girl soon."

Youichiro smiled at more than just Sasaki's absurdly misplaced concern. "No need. I already have."

"Already?"

He stretched like a cat in the back seat. "I thought I'd seen her somewhere before, so I hugged her. The shape and feel of her body, the scent of her hair, it was all exactly as I remembered. And then she admitted it." Youichiro's smile was self-satisfied, but had more warmth than usual.

"I should have transferred weeks ago, rather than wasting time with our chloroform games."

Sasaki sighed wearily. "I'm sorry you feel that way, sir."

Youichiro's smirk became a full-blown smile. "Don't tell me you've started to enjoy dragging unconscious girls into the bushes."

Sasaki softly cleared his throat in protest at the jibe. "If you have truly found her, then there is no reason to continue attending that school, is there? Let us inquire at her place of residence and be done with it."

Youichiro rubbed his pale temples and considered his options.

Clearly quite flustered, the girl had turned red and seemed on the verge of tears. The boy with the wild eyes—who Youichiro had already guessed wasn't as hard-boiled as he looked—obviously had feelings for her, jumping to her defense without a second's thought. The way he'd flushed while denying his feelings for her only proved the truth of that charge.

"I believe I shall remain enrolled, at least for the time being. Karin has not yet agreed to anything, and I have no intention of backing down from Kenta."

Sasaki grunted at the latter name. "Who is this Kenta?"

Considering how to go about approaching Karin tomorrow, Youichiro ignored him. *The first order of business is to find out whether or not she actually likes me. While it would be convenient to simply knock on her front door and ask her, girls don't operate like that.*

He never noticed Sasaki carefully studying his expression in the rearview mirror.

Karin's home was an old but well-maintained European-style building at the top of a hill. The sounds of two successively slammed doors, the front one and the one to Karin's room, were still echoing through the house when she dove on her bed in a paroxysm of sobs. This time of year, sunset was a few hours away and her family was still asleep.

"I can never go to school again!" she wailed, beating the mattress with her small fists.

What a terrible day it had been. Its only saving grace was that nobody had realized she was a vampire. Although that would have been better than what they must be thinking now!

Now they think I'm a teenaged hooker! And I can't think of any way to explain what Kenta says without telling them what was really going on. Oh, I just want to die! I want to die, die, die, die!

She'd been a keyed up and very distraught mess when she first collapsed onto the bed, with sleep the last thing on her mind, but the day had taken a physical toll on her. Her eyes fluttered once, twice, and then the world went away.

At least until a slipper bounced off her head.

"Ouch! What the . . . ?"

Her mother, Calera, was standing next to the bed, holding out Karin's school bag with the disgust of someone who'd just used rubber gloves to pick up a dead mouse the cat dragged in.

"Mama?"

"Don't just drop this in the middle of the hall. I almost tripped over it! Sure, I can see in the dark, but my eyes have to be open, and they're as bleary as yours are when I've just gotten up. Be more careful!"

Her body was sheathed in a velvety purple cocktail gown. Calera stood there with one hand on her slim hip, her ample chest thrust forward. She had the high cheekbones and patrician nose of a fashion model, but her current expression was that of an annoyed commuter who'd just sat on a chair with chewing gum stuck to it.

Looking up at her mother, Karin's eyes filled with tears.

"Oh, Mama, I can't ever go to school again!" Popping out of bed like a jack-in-the-box, she wrapped her arms around the startled Calera.

Ten minutes later, the Maaka family was gathered in the living room for a conference.

"Sure, the kidnappings in the park are dangerous," said her father, Henry. "But is it really certain that you were the target? I think you'll be fine if you avoid that area for a while."

Calera stroked her chin with violet-painted nails. "The real problem is this Youichiro Juumonji, especially if he were to remember being bitten by Karin. Fortunately, he has the wrong idea."

"That's embarrassing enough!" protested Karin. "Now everyone thinks I'm the sort of girl who throws herself at complete strangers!"

"And what's wrong with that?" asked her brother Ren with apparent surprise.

"You might be like that, but not me!" snapped Karin.

Her horn-dog brother rarely came home except to sleep, preferring to spend his nights with whatever woman he'd seduced that week. He wasn't exactly someone to whom Karin looked for moral guidance.

"I'd rather everyone knew I was a vampire than think I'm a teen prostitute!"

Her parents and her brother all hissed at once. "Don't say that!"

Karin fell quiet.

Everyone glanced at one another.

Leave it to her little sister Anju to deliver the most cutting remark: "Don't be stupid. Either way, people would be thinking you're something you're not, and believing you to be a slut puts the family in less danger than if they believed you to be a real vampire."

"Don't remind me!" wailed Karin from behind her hands. "That's even more embarrassing—you know how much I wish I could be like the rest of you!"

Anju's scowl softened. "He doesn't remember that you bit him, right? Then all you needed was a decent excuse. Say you were surprised by a snake and leapt on the nearest person in terror."

"Snakes are rare in the city."

Anju stomped her little foot on the carpeted floor in exasperation. "A caterpillar, then; you're wimpy enough that he'd believe you were terrified by a caterpillar."

Karin sighed wistfully. "Yeah, I guess I could have done that . . ."

"Kinda late now, Sis," snorted Ren.

Calera nodded. "Honestly, child, you're such a ninny sometimes. Now that everyone in school knows about it, it's pointless to erase his partial memory of you hugging him. Some people are pretty hard to manipulate; you ought to count yourself lucky he doesn't remember being bitten."

"Even if you don't drink the blood, you still have to bite necks just like the rest of us, so you ought to be better at it by now," said Ren in a mocking tone.

"It's just not as easy for me as it is for the rest of you," groaned Karin. "Nothing is!"

Henry stared at the ceiling in consternation, stroking his neatly groomed mustache. "But dearest," he said to his exasperated wife, "you must admit that her having a blood rush every time she gets near the boy is rather alarming! Karin's got enough problems with that Kenta Usui in her class, without having a second trigger around."

Karin nodded vigorously. "Exactly, Papa! And even if I try to avoid him, Youichiro keeps coming after me! What can I do, other than skip school?"

"You do that, he'll just come here," said Ren. "I mean, that's what I'd do, and he's probably almost as smart as me."

Everyone paused to exchange significant glances. Finally, Henry broke the uncomfortable silence. "That

"That would be unfortunate. Not that a normal human is likely to make it all the way here."

"True," said Calera, "but how many so-called normal humans are able to break even part of Anju's memory manipulation? No, we must plan for the worst contingency."

"At night we can use the bats to make people lose their way, but they won't do us much good during daylight."

Lost in her own worries, Karin tuned out the conversation. She would be far worse off if he managed to find her house. It being a vampire's lair, there were so many things just lying around that would be rather alarming to an ordinary human. Even her best friend Maki had never visited.

"So what should I do?"

Ren gave her his best smirk. "Go out with him, of course. Take one for the team."

"How can you say that?" wailed Karin.

Ren's smirk morphed into his best approximation of a patient smile. "Look, Sis, take it from the guy who knows about this stuff. The more the girl runs, the more the guy likes her—that's just how the world works. You go out with him, he'll be satisfied and never think about coming here. Besides, you date the guy, you'll get the perfect opportunity to put the bite on him. It'll just be another kind of hickey. Even if he makes your blood boil over, just bite him and your problem's solved. Maybe you'll even learn how to erase his memory, and won't need Anju anymore."

"But I've never even held hands with a boy!"

"Then it's about time you started, isn't it? You won't be such a spaz once you get the first time over and done with. Look how much cooler I became after I turned thirteen."

His mother nodded. "That's not the way I would put it, but your brother does have a point."

Karin stared at her in disbelief. Had everyone gone crazy?

"He's smart and good looking, right?" Ren continued. "Maybe not as much as me, but more so than most, right? And he's the heir to a wealthy family. Guys like that aren't exactly lining up to be your first time, but for some reason this one wants you!"

"For some reason? What's *that* supposed to mean?!"

"Calm down, Karin," said her father. "Listen to what your brother has to say."

Ren pressed on. "C'mon, a guy this good is probably never going to come along again. I'm not saying you have to marry him, just go out with him a few times. Or what, is there someone else? Is that it?"

Karin flushed, trying to banish the mental image of a certain tall boy whose sinister scowl and wild-looking eyes belied how nice he actually was.

No, what am I thinking? Sure, I was grateful for his help, but that doesn't mean I have any special feelings for Kenta!

Karin shook her head in an attempt to clear it of these strange emotions.

Ren took this as a denial. "Then what's the freaking problem? Go out with the rich pretty boy; it'll be a good experience for you." Standing up, he looked at his watch. "I gotta go. I promised Mariko I'd be back her at her place once it got dark. The girl's blood tastes *so* good, but she's crazy jealous!" Humming what Karin guessed was some recent pop song, he strode out of the room.

Calera raised and eyebrow and snorted. "Honestly, which place does that boy think is his lair, this house or some girl's apartment?"

Karin put her face in her hands. "And now you all want me to be like him!"

Her father shook his head. "That's not what we're saying. But even a broken clock is right twice a day. Ultimately, it's your decision whether or not you like this young man, but it seems like there's nothing to lose and maybe a lot to be gained by getting to know him. At the very least, you should go to school tomorrow and try to figure out what he has in mind."

Anju nodded. "Hey, it's better than him coming here during daylight."

"But everyone thinks I'm some kind of prostitute! Surely you can see that's what's so embarrassing!"

Her mother squeezed her shoulder. "Nobody who really knows you would believe that, Karin. Anju's proposed explanation may not be ideal, but it's the best you've got. Work on making people believe it. You might be surprised at how easy it is."

Unable to think of anything better, Karin nodded. "Okay, okay, I'll think about it. Right now I guess I'd better go study. It's not like my other problems have gone away while I was worrying about this."

As the single family member who wasn't nocturnal, Karin could only see her family from the time the sun went down to whenever it was she went to sleep. Although she had her own bedroom, she usually did her homework in the living room, just so that she had a little more time in their company.

Today, though, she wanted to be alone.

God, how can I look Maki in the eye tomorrow? Or worse, Kenta!

Sighing, she nodded at her parents and trudged upstairs. Once she was in her room, she made to shut the door behind her, but met with resistance. Anju had followed her.

"What do you want?" Karin asked.

Anju looked more solemn than usual. "Oh, I was just going back to my room as well. But first, I was wondering about your classmate Kenta. The one who makes your blood scream?"

Karin sat down, feeling even more overwhelmed. "What about him? My blood still rises every time I get near him, but it's no longer at tsunami levels."

Besides just getting her life back in order, she'd desperately wanted to make Kenta happy. But rather than doing that, she'd caused him even more trouble.

He tried to help me again today. Sure made a mess of things, though. Maybe we're more alike than I thought. Remembering how his white shirt had suddenly appeared in her blurred vision like a shield, she felt her cheeks burning.

Anju looked at her oddly "What's the matter?"

"Nothing. Well, nothing but Youichiro."

"Will you go out with him?"

"I don't know. I mean, I can't just . . ." Unable to find the words, she threw up her hands.

As much as she didn't want to admit it, her brother had an obvious point when he'd said Youichiro would make an ideal boyfriend. How many things in her life had ever been ideal?

I can see why everybody was raving about how cool he is, like a prince in a fairy tale. So why don't I want to go out with him?

Yet when she thought about being hugged by him, her heart beat faster.

He smelled like green citrus. Must be some kind of cologne. His arms went right around me. He looks slim, but those arms were so strong, and he was so tall. When I looked up at his face, my heart beat faster and my body got all hot. It was hard to breathe.

And she'd wanted to bite him. Ultimately, it came down to that.

Dejected, Karin rested her head on her hands. She'd been embraced by a boy as good looking as any magazine model or movie star she'd ever seen, yet her reaction was so unromantic.

What was it about Youichiro that made her blood go off? That smooth confidence and self-satisfied arrogance hardly seemed like someone who was unhappy.

"Karin?"

She looked up at her sister. "Yeah?"

"I know I agreed with Ren earlier, but now I'm thinking maybe you shouldn't go out with this Youichiro after all," said Anju gravely, sounding like someone much older than she actually was. "I'm afraid he'll get tired of you pretty quick and toss you aside."

"So on top of everything else, I'm destined to be dumped?"

"You think otherwise?"

Karin shrugged in defeat. "Yeah, that would be just my luck."

There was no logical reason why he'd chosen her to begin with. It must have been some bizarre whim, which meant that there was a good chance he'd come to his senses and dump her just as fast as he'd fallen for her.

"I'm pretty sure you would . . ." Anju's voice trailed off as she thought better of whatever it was she'd meant to say. "Never mind, Sis. I know you must need your sleep. Worry about this when you're feeling better. Good night." Giving the silent Karin a mysterious smile, she retreated back to her room.

It rained the next day. Many students clumped together, chatting under shared umbrellas, while others splashed past them on bicycles, protected by dripping raincoats.

"Morning!"

"Hey. Guess we're inside for gym today."

"So much rain!"

"That's a new umbrella, isn't it? Nice color!"

As Karin passed through the gates, she saw some girls from her class. "Hello, Chika, Yukari. Good morning!"

But they didn't reply. After glaring at Karin for a moment, they whispered something to each other and hurried inside the building.

She stood there in the rain, not wanting to follow them but not having much choice. *Please don't let the rest of the day be like this!*

Things weren't any better inside. Just walking down the hall, she got glared at by those students who bothered to look at her at all.

But then someone took her arm. It was her best friend, smiling a smile that belied the concern in her eyes.

"Morning, Maki. Yikes, I'm so wet!"

Her friend hugged her. "I don't care about that. To heck with the rain. And to heck with those idiots who say . . ." She caught herself, not willing to complete the sentence.

"Who say . . . what?"

"Nothing, it doesn't matter."

"Who says I've been prostituting myself?"

The look in Maki's eyes told her all she needed to know. So much for her mother's naive suggestion that nobody who knew her would believe it.

Maki sighed. "Well, you brought it up, not me. I heard about it from a girl who came to practice late. She said the hot new transfer student cornered you in the hall, wrapped his arms around you, and kissed you right on the mouth? That true?"

Karin could only stare at her friend.

"Then she said it wasn't the first time you'd come on to him, and that Kenta was all pissed about you cheating and the two of them had a big fistfight in the hall."

Karin made a strangled sound that was her best approximation of a scornful laugh. "That is so ridiculous!" Hoping that her suddenly hot face wasn't contradicting her words, she tried to explain what had really happened. But how much did she actually know? She'd run away in the middle of the confrontation, so maybe there really *had* been a fistfight! Regardless, it was obvious the story was taking on a life of its own.

"Sure, I really did grab onto Youichiro in the nature park, but that was, um, because I got scared by a snake, not because I was turning tricks or anything disgusting like that!"

"A snake? In the nature park?"

"Okay, maybe it was a caterpillar, the point is, I was so scared!"

Maki actually looked convinced, which made Karin feel bad about lying, especially when her friend hugged her again. "Oh, sweetie, don't cry! I know you could never do anything like that!"

Karin wiped her eyes on her sleeve. It was just too embarrassing. And while Maki obviously meant well, what she said next only made her feel worse. "So Asako and her friends are pretty pissed. They thought that boy was some kind of prince and now they're going on like you seduced him! They're so darn stupid!"

"But how can they think that?"

Letting go of her, Maki shrugged. "Ah, they're just jealous, that's all. Still, you should maybe watch out."

They'd reached the door to Class 1-D. When Karin opened it and walked to her seat, she gasped in horror. Her desk was covered in flyers for escort services and telephone chat lines.

"What is this!" she cried as she peeled them off and wadded them up.

A mocking voice came from behind her. "Gee, Maaka, I thought you were looking for extra work. Those all seem right up your alley."

It was Asako, sitting at her desk, surrounded by several of her friends. They all looked at Karin and sniggered.

Maki shook her fist at them. "Did you do this?"

Asako made a theatrical attempt at looking offended. "Goodness gracious, no. Those flyers were here when we got here, right, girls?"

"I figured Maaka had left them behind," said one with infuriating nonchalance.

"We heard she uses those places all the time," said another, more openly sneering.

"But that's just not true!" snapped Maki, squeezing Karin's shoulder. "C'mon, you tell them how stupid they're being!"

Stammering, Karin struggled to formulate a defense. "Yeah, sure, I put my arms around him in the park, but that's because I was surprised by a snake . . ."

"What a good trick for seducing men! Ha ha!" laughed another. "I guess we'll have to remember that one!"

Karin wanted to cry. The fact that she was lying to them just made it harder.

Maki leapt to her defense again. "Get over yourselves! You're just jealous, which is so sad. Instead of picking on poor Karin, maybe you should've asked the new guy out yourselves!"

Asako flushed at the word "jealous." Maki had hit the nail on the head.

Someone applauded from the doorway. "Nice one, Tokitou." Fukumi Naitou, who'd clearly heard the tail end of the conversation, entered the room. Coming over to Karin, she patted her lightly on the back. "Who cares about gossip? You haven't done anything wrong, Maaka, so stop acting guilty." Despite the admonition, her tone was kind.

Knowing that she had allies besides Maki gave Karin strength. She glared at the girls who'd been gossiping about her. Realizing that not everyone in the room was going to follow their example, Asako and Chika wilted under her stare. Around them, more than one member of their little clique looked ashamed of herself.

If that had been the end of it, Karin's life might have gone back to normal. But then the classroom door opened again and the room was filled with the scent of roses.

Upon looking up, Karin nearly fell out of her chair. There was Youichiro Juumonji, carrying the biggest bouquet of roses she'd ever seen. Her face immediately turned as red as the blossoms.

This was all so wrong; as wrong as it was possible for things to be on an ordinary Monday morning in an ordinary public high school. Karin stared at Youichiro, open-mouthed. *Everybody* stared at him.

Yet he remained as unconcerned as an adult gawked at by a roomful of toddlers. Striding straight to Karin, he presented her with the roses, not with a princely flourish, but as matter-of-factly as someone doing the most natural thing in the world.

"Good morning, Karin!" He didn't grin, didn't smirk, didn't look coy. His expression and tone were those of someone nodding at a neighbor or buying something from a shop clerk.

Karin glanced over, hoping for moral support, but Maki was gone. She hadn't flinched when standing up to Asako and her cronies, but she'd been overwhelmed by Youichiro's obliviousness to everyone and everything but the roses in his hand and the girl he was giving them to, and so she'd retreated into the ring of spectators.

Abandoned, Karin searched for a response. "Um, good roses—I mean, morning. Are these for . . . for . . . me?" The last word of that stammered sentence was barely audible.

Youichiro nodded. "I wasn't sure what you actually liked, but roses seemed a safe choice. If you don't like them, feel free to throw them away."

"N-n-no, I don't have anything against roses, they're fine, just fine, r-r-really."

There were so many that the blood-colored blooms would spill over her desk and onto the floor if he actually put them down in front of her. Karin had no idea what to do with them, but refusing them wasn't much of an option.

"Thank you, but I don't have any place to put them."

He shrugged. "Give them to your driver? Or did your car already leave?"

She stared at him for a moment, trying to figure out what he was talking about. Then it dawned on her that he must think that everyone was driven to school by a chauffeur. Under other circumstances, that would have made her laugh, but right then she couldn't remember how.

"I don't have a car," she finally said, wondering why it felt like an almost shameful confession. "I walk to school."

His expression wasn't scornful or contemptuous, but that of an anthropologist observing some fascinating tribal ritual. "Every day?"

She nodded. "Every day."

"You must have very strong legs for a girl."

Her face tingled at the thought of him thinking about her legs. "No more than anybody else's."

He nodded. "A whole school of pedestrians. Come to think of it, Sasaki said that most students don't use cars. I guess they must really care about the environment." It was the first time she'd seen him look impressed.

His eyes focused back on Karin. "My sincere apologies for yesterday. I shouldn't have embraced you like that, not without some kind of warning, or at least a bit more of an introduction. Because of the incident in the park, I was under the impression you had a crush on me. I'm sorry if I was wrong, but I couldn't think of another reason why you would do that."

Karin glanced down at the roses and mumbled her rehearsed excuse.

"There was this snake—I was so scared . . ."

He raised a delicate eyebrow. "A snake? What of the other incidents that Kenta mentioned? He said he saw you hugging other people."

She raised her hand to her mouth. "I'm so bad with snakes. And caterpillars. And worms. Or anything that looks like a snake, even toy ones. One time there was this garden hose . . ."

"It's not good to be so afraid of things," he said in a grave but not unsympathetic voice. "Especially things that can't hurt you."

Karin had never been good at lying. The best liars knew no shame and she had enough of that to spare. She looked at the floor. "I know, but sometimes I just . . . I just panic, that's all, and before I know it, I grab onto the nearest person."

Her discomfort apparently made the lie more convincing, for Youichiro sighed and said, "So that was it. The truth is often so much more ordinary than what we assume."

Karin nodded with exaggerated enthusiasm. "I'm ordinary. I'm very, very ordinary."

Youichiro looked at her solemnly. "I don't believe that, but it would make it easier, I suppose."

Yes, thought Karin to herself, *it would make everything so much easier*. "What do you mean?"

"I'm going to have to make you fall me in love with me," said Youichiro as matter-of-factly as if he'd remarked on the weather. "I suppose that the more ordinary you are, the easier that task would be, but I don't really believe you *are* ordinary."

Karin could only stare at him. Any other time, she might have been worried, but what he'd said right before that drove all other thoughts from her head.

"I wish to formally request that we continue our association," he continued in the same matter-of-fact tone.

Of course, she hadn't been the only one listening. The room practically exploded. There were more than a few cheers and whistles.

It was so strange, she couldn't even be shocked. "This is, um, very sudden."

"It's been three months since we first met. Surely that's time enough."

"Well, yeah, that's, um, yeah, that's just . . ."

Anything else she might have said was drowned by renewed noise from the onlookers. Kenta Usui had come in through the back door. The surrounding murmur stopped just as quickly as it had begun. Everyone was watching, as transfixed as spectators at a play—or a prize fight.

The warm smile that so contrasted with Kenta's gangster eyes faded. "Hell—" he said, looking from Karin to Youichiro to the huge pile of roses. He wasn't cursing; surprise had cut him off in mid-hello.

Karin had fled before being able to hear Youichiro challenge Kenta the day before, but there was no misunderstanding the electric tension that crackled between them. Her heartbeat accelerated. Anxiety twisted every fiber of her being.

Kenta stalked wordlessly to his seat, plopped his bag down, and stomped right back out of the room. Except when displaying a rare smile, his wasn't the friendliest of faces. Now it was a mask of samurai ferocity. The door slamming shut behind him didn't break the silence of the onlookers. As for Karin, she felt as though she'd turned to stone.

Either Youichiro was oblivious to all this drama, or he just didn't care. "For someone who claims to be your classmate and not your boyfriend, he certainly seems upset," he said, managing to sound even more dryly matter-of-fact than before.

"Well, he's not!" said Karin, feeling herself beginning to sweat. "He's nothing like that."

"Then we need pay him no attention. May I have your answer?"

She blinked as if trying to make a hallucination go away. "Um, um, um . . ."

The warning bell rang.

"Ah, we're out of time," said Youichiro, turning on his heel. "I'll see you later."

Karin realized she was still holding the flowers. "Hey! I mean, I'm so sorry, but you can't just stick me with these. I've got nowhere to put them!"

"Throw them away if you don't want them," he said with no trace of irritation. "They belong to you now."

"B-b-but I can't do that; it wouldn't be right!"

It was too late. Youichiro was gone and Karin was left standing there, holding the bouquet. Spinning around in the vain of hope of finding moral support, she found herself transfixed by the icy stares of Asako and her cronies.

Eeek! They sure don't look happy!

"Your prince has such bad timing," sighed Fukumi.

"Yeah, just when it looked like things were going to be cool," agreed Maki, glancing at the door through which Youichiro had just exited.

Yet Maki's attack on Asako's jealousy apparently had some impact. She and her clique continued to glare, but not one of them said a word to Karin for the rest of the morning, which proceeded without incident once Karin overcame her embarrassment.

"I hope I shamed them into keeping their mouths shut," said Maki quietly as she and Karin ate their lunches in the classroom.

The bouquet of roses was too large, so after the morning homeroom, she had passed it over to their teacher, Professor Shirai, who had taken it to the staff room. Things sort of settled down after that.

"I hope so too," said Karin, still uncomfortable about the whole scene and pretending to concentrate on her food.

"Not everyone thinks like Asako. Fukumi was right; you need to carry on like it's nothing."

Looking up from her food, Karin smiled for the first time that day. "Thanks."

"For what?"

"For sticking up for me. If not for you, I would have run home crying."

"That's what friends are for," said Maki, deftly swiping the egg from Karin's bento box.

"That and stealing food, apparently!" But given what Maki had done for her, she couldn't begrudge the girl an egg. Putting the bento box away, Karin took out a textbook and answer sheet. "Can you help me with fifth period math? He ended in the row next to me yesterday, so I'm sure he's going to call on me today."

Maki nodded. "He goes in order—you'll probably get problem number two."

Karen slumped in her chair. "Which I don't understand it at all! Those two weeks off are killing me."

"It's not just the time you took off," said Maki with a grimace. "I didn't get it either. Maybe you can ask Kenta? I think he's in the cafeteria."

Karin felt her cheeks burning again. "Why Kenta?"

Maki shrugged. "He got a good score on the last quiz and always seems to know the answer when he gets called on, so I guess he must be pretty smart." She lowered her voice. "Honestly now, what do you really think of him?"

Karin tried to keep a poker face, but she could feel her heart beating faster. "He's just a classmate. And a coworker."

Maki looked unconvinced. "I'm just saying, that boy's got feelings for you! Yesterday, he was sitting next to Fukumi when I was telling her how you fell down the stairs. You should have seen those eyebrows of his start twitching! You know what a stone face he usually is—even when Maeda's test tube exploded and he got chemicals and glass in his hair, his expression didn't change. But when the boy heard about you, he looked *worried*."

Karin stared at the floor like someone was projecting a really interesting movie down there. "Must be a coincidence," she mumbled.

Maki lowered her voice another notch. "If you don't think of him as anything more than a friend, so be it. But what about the prince?"

"The prince?"

"That's what everybody's calling Mister Hottie Transfer Student now. Can you think of a better nickname, what with those looks, that personality and all that money?"

Now Karin was staring at the floor like she hoped a trapdoor was going to appear there, one she could crawl through. "It fits, I guess."

"Well? What about him?"

Now she almost wished that Maki had left her to freak out and go running home. "I don't know! I never even spoke to him before yesterday. What am I gonna say to him?"

Maki sighed. "I'm not good with stuck-up people, so I don't care who he hooks up with. But a lot of girls can't resist those dreamy looks, and for most of them, the attitude only makes him hotter. They're crazy to catch his eye, Asako being the craziest. You drag this out, she's gonna hate you for sure. If you're going to go out with him, do it! Otherwise tell him you're not interested. But either way, make a decision."

What was it her brother had said? Something about how boys like him weren't exactly lining up to ask her out. He'd told her to go for it.

Sure, he's all haughty and arrogant, but that's how princes are supposed to be, and what girl doesn't want to date a prince? Besides, I think maybe he's a pretty nice person under that spoiled attitude. And he's so good looking! But surely that's not enough reason to go out with someone I don't even know!

She was of two minds about the prospect, and they were starting to get into a shoving match with each other.

"Karin, why are you drawing a spiral on your answer sheet?"

She looked down at the pattern she'd been scribbling with her mechanical pencil. It reflected the way her thoughts had been spinning round and round. As she erased it, someone came in the door behind her.

Maki shrank back into her seat. "He's here again."

He who? But she knew who it had to be.

She looked up. Yep, just as she feared, Youichiro Juumonji was striding straight to Karin's seat with that nonchalant, male model strut of his.

"I thought perhaps you had an answer to this morning's question." Then, as if uncharacteristically aware of being rude, he nodded at Maki. "You are . . . Karin's friend?"

Maki stood up with a strained smile. "I am, but I have a name, too. But I'm sure you've got better things to do than learn it."

Youichiro's face displayed no rancor at the jibe. "Pardon me, I meant no offense."

Maki flushed. Karin knew her well enough to suspect she wasn't so much embarrassed as irritated at finding herself intimidated by Youichiro's princely aura. Maki looked down at a wadded-up sandwich wrapper in her hand. "I think I'll just go throw this away. I've got a couple of things to do before next class, so I'll talk to you in a bit, Karin. Good luck." She squeezed her friend's shoulder and nodded at Youichiro. "Nice to meet you, Your Highness."

Maki, wait! Don't leave me alone!

Youichiro settled gracefully in Maki's vacant seat. "Well, let's have it." His tone of voice was less brusque than the words, but that didn't help much.

"Hold on, we can't talk about that now!"

Youichiro seemed to know so little about everyday social graces that he might as well have been a robot or an alien. Maki hadn't exactly left them alone together—due to the rain, the room was even more crowded than usual for lunchtime.

But as he'd said the day before, he simply didn't care who else was listening. "You haven't decided?"

Karin both nodded and shook her head. "Yes. I mean, no. No, I haven't. I'm sorry, it's just . . . it's just all so sudden, and well, can you give me more time?"

Youichiro's face remained impassive. For all his hauteur, he didn't seem prone to pouting or acting put out. "Of course. It's wise of you not to make such decisions lightly. I'm glad to see you're not as rash and impulsive as I mistakenly assumed."

Did that mean he was glad to realize she wasn't a slut? That was something, at least. Now if only she could convince everyone else.

"So, we won't worry about that right now. Let's just talk."

"What, here?"

"Why not?"

She couldn't talk where everyone was listening, but if they went somewhere else, she was pretty sure everybody else in the room would just follow, along with whoever saw them in the hall.

What can I do? I don't think Maki's coming back . . .

Karin found her excuse in the answer sheet spread out on her desk.

"Well, see, I still haven't done my homework for fifth period math. I'm probably going to have to demonstrate this problem during class, so I need to figure it out before the end of break."

Youichiro glanced down at her notes. He raised one delicate eyebrow, not at all like Kenta's caterpillar bristle.

"Rather an easy problem," he said airily.

Karin hung her head. It might be easy for a senior, but she'd been struggling with it all night and gotten nowhere.

"Problem one: A is four, B is two."

"Huh?"

He tapped the answer sheet. "Problem two: the straight line AB's equation is Y equals X plus twelve. Problem three: the minimal value is . . ."

Despite looking at the problems upside down, Youichiro's voice never faltered. It was not surprising that a third-year student could solve a first year student's math homework, but not *this* fast! He was rattling off all the answers in a completely relaxed manner.

Waving for him to stop, Karin snatched up a pencil. "Wait, wait! Let me write this down!"

People all around the room were doing the same. Karin was clearly not the only one who hadn't finished.

"Okay, go on."

"Problem one: A is four, B is two. Problem two: the straight line AB's equation is . . ."

"But the work for problem one?"

"Symmetric transformation of that graph."

Karin blinked. "Sorry, could you be a little more detailed?"

"I'm sure you know how to transform it over the X axis, so just . . . Oh, wait, you *don't* know how, do you?"

Youichiro could clearly solve all these problems in his head. He had to be some sort of genius, so his explanations tended to leave out a lot of important information. But as

Karin asked away and he repeated himself in more detail, he gradually taught her the problem one step at a time.

"And that's why A equals four, and B equals two."

"Oh. Sorry, I'm so stupid!"

"Not at all. I'm aware my explanations are hard to understand. At my old school, one of my friends got angry with me, shouting, 'Don't make fun of me! Explain it so I can understand!' I hadn't done it intentionally, so I didn't know why he got so angry." Youichiro sighed and looked almost wistful, but when Karin blinked, his familiar mask had returned.

She felt a twinge of sympathy. "I know! My brother is always yelling at me for needing my sister's help, but it's not like I ask it just to inconvenience her! If I could do it myself, I would. Sometimes it makes me want to cry that I can't."

In one sense, they were complete opposites; Youichiro was yelled at for being too smart and thus unable to explain things properly, while Karin was yelled at for being defective and not having enough powers. But they were both yelled at for things they had no control over. When she looked at it that way, the gulf between them didn't seem to wide.

Was that a crinkle around Youichiro's eyes? "It makes you want to cry? That means you're a good person."

Karin's heart skipped a beat. *Is he . . . smiling? Wow, he really does look like a prince!*

It wasn't that she hadn't thought him gorgeous before, but it had been in an abstract way, like a painting in a museum. His high-handed and distant attitude hadn't annoyed her, exactly, but it had kept her from feeling the full effect of his good looks. Until now.

He's smart, he's being really nice about helping me—can someone this great really be asking me to go out with him?

Karin stole a glance up at him, as if taking him in for the first time.

"Anyway, my friend got so mad," continued Youichiro, oblivious to the way she'd just checked him out. "All I did was tell him that if he would shut up and actually listen to what I'd just said before asking me to repeat myself, maybe it wouldn't feel like I was trying to explain brain surgery to a monkey. Somehow, that turned into a fight."

"Wow, imagine that!"

A couple of people around them snickered, suggesting that Karin wasn't the only one not surprised that his friend had gotten mad at him. As usual, he remained oblivious to all that.

"The point is, if you don't understand it, then just sit down and graph it out. Do that enough times and you'll soon be able to graph similar problems in your head. Once you do that, it all becomes very easy."

"Really?" It at least sounded like it might work.

"That's what they told me at my last school," continued Youichiro impatiently. "I could do it without drawing a graph in the first place, so I've no idea if it's true. Problem two?" He wasn't bragging or showing off, just stating the truth as he perceived it.

As she carefully wrote down everything he taught her, Karin thought about how nobody was ever just one thing. *Sure, he can cause problems, but he's not a bad person. Maybe he's stuc- up, but he's also genuinely nice.*

Just as they finished her homework, the speaker above the blackboard crackled to life. "Youichiro Juumonji, of

3-A, please come to the teacher's room. Once again, 3-A, Juumonji. Please come to the teacher's room."

Karin looked up at her new tutor with concern. "Did something happen?"

He shrugged. "Might be about me telling the third-period English teacher his pronunciation was dreadful. Can't think of anything else offhand." He stood up. "See you after school?"

"Well, see, I have to run right home today and get changed for work. Sorry!"

He nodded. "Well, if you have a prior engagement . . ."

Why did she feel guilty? "I *am* sorry. And the flowers were too big for the classroom, so the teacher took them to the staff office. I felt bad, since you went to all the trouble of buying them, but they really were nice!"

Karin bowed her head. When he'd handed them over that morning, she was too worried about what to do with so many roses to take pleasure in them, but now that he'd helped her with her homework, she felt like a rat.

"Forget it. I was thoughtless. From now on I shall have them delivered to your home. See you tomorrow." Was that another trace of a smile he flashed at her before heading toward the door?

Of course, he *would* be leaving just as Kenta Usui was coming back in. Karin's bad luck wasn't going to desert her any time soon.

The two boys froze for a moment, staring at each other like alley cats.

Youichiro allowed a small smile to play across his lips. Had there been a course on how to piss other people off, that expression would have earned him the highest possible grade.

"I beg your pardon," he said with mock civility as he slipped past Kenta and out the door.

Kenta glared after him for a moment, then stalked to his own seat, yanked the chair back, and sat down heavily. He pointedly avoided looking at Karin.

But everyone else did, then looked back at him, and then at her again. From the surrounding murmurs, she picked out the words "jealous," "rival," and "triangle."

But that's not true, she wanted to shout. *It's nothing like that!*

Karin buried her face in her hands.

"See you tomorrow, Maki."

"Bye-bye, Karin. Good luck at work!"

The final class of the day was over. Maki went off to practice while Karin headed toward the bathroom. Today she had to work at Julian, the family restaurant. There was only one staff toilet there and it could get pretty crowded during shift changes, so she'd decided to take care of business before leaving school grounds. Afterward, she washed her hands, straightened her uniform and checked herself out in the mirror. Her last class of the day was gym, and once she'd hurried straight to work without noticing that several of her buttons were undone. When a coworker made a joke about it, she'd been so embarrassed she'd almost cried.

Clothes are fine; hair is fine; everything's good.

Just as she was about to leave, she heard familiar voices approaching from the hall. It was Chika and Asako, looking just as surprised as Karin felt. But they quickly scowled and advanced on her.

"Just the person I wanted to see," said Asako with a supercilious purr.

"Hey, sorry, but I'm kind of in a hurry here . . ."

"I bet she has a date," said Asako with a sneer.

"Yeah," said Chika just as snidely, "Little Miss Busy Bee sure seems to find the time for *that,* despite all her talk of makeup tests."

"No, no, I have to work!" said Karin, trying unsuccessfully to slip past them.

They blocked her.

"Now what kind of work could that be? Chika, you hold her here while I go get the others."

"Others?" Karin gulped.

Chika had a tight grip on her arm. "That's right, Karin, we aren't the only ones who want a word with you. You don't just give yourself a bad name by whoring yourself out, but the school suffers as well."

She was too shocked to try to break Chika's grip. "But I haven't done anything!"

"Yeah, right, other than make out with businessmen and jump total strangers in the park!"

Karin might have been able to break free, but Asako was already back with half a dozen older girls. The sheer mass of them shoved Karin back against the wall.

"So Little Miss Mousey here is the prostitue I've been hearing so much about?"

"You have the nerve to show your face here, after everyone found out about you yesterday?"

"If the papers get ahold of this, you know there'll be trouble for all of us. We can't have you dragging us down into the mud with you. You need to leave here and never come back!"

Their voices were an accusatory chorus echoing off the tiles. A first-year girl started to come in, but turned on her heel and fled when she saw what was going on.

Karin desperately tried to defend herself through rational argument. "No, no, you don't understand! Yes, I hugged him in the park but that was just . . ." Before she could launch into her story about the snake, they shouted her down.

"So you admit it, you brazen little hussy!"

"How dare you! I'm in the same class as him and I've barely spoken to him at all!"

"You handed off the flowers to the teacher, then called him over at lunch and made him do your homework—I bet you think you've got him twisted around your little finger, you tramp!"

"Girl, you're out of your league. If you don't believe me, just take a look in that mirror."

"Sluts like you think they can have anybody you want, but you aren't getting him, you ugly little freshman skank!"

"Yeah, not if we have anything to say about it!"

It was obvious that their accusations of prostitution were just a cover for their jealousy. Youichiro's interest in her was their real beef, not the alleged disgrace that she was bringing their school. This could get very, very ugly. She twisted in their grip, struggling to break free.

"Let go of me!" Karin had always been a shy, sweet girl, not a scrappy tomboy—the age differences between her and Ren and Anju meant that she'd never even brawled with her siblings, as was common in some families. Should she try to kick her tormentors in the shins, or would that only make things worse?

"You're not going anywhere yet, not 'til we're done with you!"

RIIIIIIIP!

In the struggle, the left sleeve of her blouse was torn halfway off! The girls surrounding her laughed at her distress.

"What was it they used to do with sluts in other countries? Strip 'em naked? Tar and feather 'em?"

Asako was probably just trying to scare her, at least with the "tar and feather" part, since neither of those items were on hand. Still, when this kind of mob mentality took over, anything could happen. Karin filled her lungs for a scream, but a louder, sharper noise cut her off.

RIIIIIIIING!

Someone had set off a fire alarm—from the hall right outside the bathroom, judging from the sound of it.

"What the hell?" Her captors stared at each other. "This isn't finals week." While their school wasn't as bad about it as some, false alarms and even bomb threats weren't unknown at exam time.

The alarm continued to sound. Whether it was a prank or a real fire, a teacher would be checking the bathroom at any moment.

"Don't think this is over, bitch!" snapped Chika as the girls filed out.

Karin slumped to the floor in relief, her heart pounding more loudly in her head than the alarm. After a moment, she collected herself and made her way unsteadily to the door.

The hall appeared to be empty, but before she could proceed to the exit, she heard a low whistle from behind her. Kenta Usui stepped out from behind a column. Despite those piercing eyes and that semi-permanent scowl, he looked relieved.

"You okay? I was pretty sure it was you they were ganging up on in there."

"How did you know?" He didn't seem like the kind of perv who would be eavesdropping outside the girls' restroom.

"I was . . . erm . . . occupied in the boy's room. Either they were very loud or that wall is very thin, because I pretty much heard everything, even though I wasn't trying to." He looked embarrassed.

"Then it was you who set off the alarm!"

He looked even more embarrassed. "Yeah, it was the only thing I could think of to do."

Once again, he'd rescued her. The tension left her body, almost as if it was flowing out from between her toes and into the linoleum floor. She blinked away the fresh moisture in her eyes.

Kenta looked away, scratching his chin. "I'm glad you're safe, but we can't hang around here, a teacher's sure to be . . ." He broke off, staring at her left shoulder.

"What?"

She glanced down. The torn seam exposed her bra strap.

"Yikes, stop looking!" Bolting on unsteady legs, she staggered down the hall.

I can't believe Kenta saw that!

He tried to keep up. "Karin, wait! It's not like I haven't seen it before!" He was referring to those occasions when she wore a sleeveless top, but it sounded worse than he meant, spurring her flight.

Like many embarrassed people, Karin panicked. Doing that while running full out can often lead to accidents. It wasn't surprising that she ran headlong into someone, rebounded, and landed flat on her butt.

"Ouch!"

"Hello, Karin."

The voice was dreadfully familiar. She looked up at Youichiro Juumonji's amused face. He helped her up, his expression changing as he noticed her torn uniform. "What happened here?

Omigod, what's he gonna think?

Even though there wasn't really a fire, her body felt enveloped in waves of heat.

Following her usual instinct, she tried to leap up and run away, but those pesky legs of hers got entangled and she went down again, face-first this time, which gave the boys another panty flash.

Youichiro knelt beside her, a large white handkerchief in his hand, like something a magician would turn into a dove. He tied it around her shoulder like a scarf, then helped her to her feet.

"Th-thanks." She straightened her uniform, her heart calming a bit now that she no longer felt exposed. But the calm didn't last long. Why was Youichiro looking so fierce? He was looking past her with a fierce glare more characteristic of Kenta than the arrogant serenity typical of his features.

"You contemptible bastard."

She looked behind her. It was appropriate that he was glaring like Kenta Usui, since that's whom he was apparently addressing. The latter had caught up to her, panting from his exertion.

No dummy, Kenta immediately realized what this must look like. His face reddened, shifting from annoyance to alarm. "Hey, I didn't do anything!"

Youichiro shook his head in disgust. "Her clothes just tore themselves, then? And you were accusing me of sexual harassment only yesterday, you hypocrite. You knew you couldn't win her from me by charm, so you tried to take her by force."

"I said I didn't do anything, dammit!"

Of course they had an audience by now.

"Karin, tell them I didn't do anything!"

Karin was so wracked by embarrassment she could barely speak. "Youichiro, this isn't what you think, really!"

His hand still on her arm, he steered her toward the door. "It's over now, so there's no need to speak of it. I'll drive you home."

Home! Yes, that would be good. She couldn't go to work like this, and his chauffeur could get her there much faster than she could run. He led her out of the school, his hand on her shoulders. It was only after they'd passed through the outer door that she thought of what she'd just done to poor Kenta.

Oh, no, I've gotten him in trouble again! I suck.

Trotting to keep up with Youichiro's long legs, she risked tripping by glancing behind her. But there were too many people, and Kenta was already out of sight.

THE BLOOD INJECTOR HAS MUCH TO WORRY ABOUT

There was a silver-white Benz parked in front of the school gates. When Youichiro emerged, the driver quickly leapt out of the seat and held the back door open for him.

He waved Karin in with one hand, then got in behind her.

"Nakaoka, we're going by her house first. Where do you live? Or would you rather I dropped you at work?"

"No, I want to go home and change first. I live in the western district. You can just drop me off nearby."

If they dropped her off in front of her house, her mother would have the vampiric equivalent of a cow, although it was more likely they'd get caught in one of the traps set up to keep humans away and never make it there.

The car ran so smoothly she hadn't even noticed when it had started moving. His lower lip quivering a bit, Youichiro looked at her. "Are you hurt? However carried away he became, I never thought he would hurt you."

"No, no, Kenta didn't do this," she finally explained, mentally kicking herself for being incoherent in the hallway. "A bunch of the older girls ganged up on me in the bathroom. He actually saved me from them!"

"Then why were you running?"

"B-because, well, it's just so embarrassing, being seen like this!" Karin hung her head.

Youichiro blinked, apparently a bit embarrassed himself, although his pale skin remained unflushed. "I jumped to conclusions, then? I'll have to apologize to him tomorrow."

"Sorry. I tried to tell you. Sometimes when I'm upset, my tongue gets all twisted up."

"It's hardly your fault. I have a bad habit of not listening to other people." Her bemusement at his self-awareness apparently showed on her face, for he looked away unhappily. "Yes, I know my own flaws. My father explained them often."

" 'Explained'?" The past tense seemed significant.

Youichiro's gaze shifted quickly from Karin to the window and back to Karin. "I hadn't planned to tell you until we were closer, but I suppose it's better if you know."

"Know what, Youichiro?"

"My father's in the hospital. Two months ago, he was in a car accident, one serious enough that there were false reports in the news. 'Juumonji Group Chairman in Fatal Accident!' It was a pretty major story—you don't remember?"

She didn't remember hearing about it, but the dealings of the rich and famous hadn't had much bearing on her own life, so she wouldn't have paid it much attention. Not that she could say *that*. "But if he's in the hospital, he's okay, right?"

"Karin, that was months ago and he's *still* there."

"Oh."

Youichiro's voice softened. "I didn't mean to snap at you. He's in a coma."

She wanted to squeeze his hand, but wasn't sure if it would be appropriate. "I'm so sorry."

"Most of the chairmen are old men appointed as decorative figureheads. Not my father. He's less than fifty years old and very active in the business. The Juumonji Group revolved around him. Without him, it can barely function."

"No one in your family can take over?"

"I have an uncle, but he's like a wart on my father's *elbow.*" The last word had the same vehemence that a less-refined person might have used for "ass."

"He has no passion for administration nor capacity for judgment. He has no creativity, no intuition, no inspiration. But he loves to make himself look important. Since I'm not of legal age, he's calling himself my guardian and has moved into the mansion. Were the law not on his side, I'd have thrown him out already—with my own hands, if necessary."

Intimidated by the sharp edge in his voice, Karin stammered, "That sounds, um, just awful. Your mother, she must be really upset."

"My mother left for Europe just before my father's accident. They'd not been a real couple for some time before that. I don't know what she's doing, where she is, or how to get in touch with her. That's why it was so easy for my uncle to worm his way into the house."

Karin's own parents, Henry and Calera, had their disagreements—which usually ended with her father yielding to her mother's bullying—but they were still a normal, functioning family and they truly loved each other. Nothing in her background gave Karin the experience to usefully respond to something like this.

Youichiro carried on analytically, as if making a formal argument in class. "Japanese medicine is among the best in the world. We've got the most skilled doctors attending my dad, but he shows no sign of waking up. As an only child, I have no one to ask for help except the gods of fortune."

Karin got it now. Yes, a boy like this could be just as unhappy as anyone else. Or even much unhappier.

She thought about her own family. Her mother had her father pretty whipped, but they were still devoted to each other. And despite their insistence on the shame of her defect, whenever she was in trouble they banded together to save her. There was nothing like that for Youichiro Juumonji. He was poor where she was rich.

The thought made her circulatory system scream.

Her heart went off, screaming like the fire alarm from earlier. Blood rushed through her veins with incredible force, almost bursting the arterial walls. Her skin felt so hot that her sweat should have been coming off it as steam.

No, not here! Yes, I'm sitting next to an unhappy person, but I'm in the middle of a serious conversation! This makes me feel like a vulture gossip columnist swooping down on a juicy rumor!

Karin desperately fought off the urge to bite him and inject him with her rising blood.

"Karin, I must ask you something."

His forceful tone took her aback. "Y-yes?"

"Do you remember embracing me once before?"

Karin hung her head as low as it would go.

Argh, I can't admit to that twice!

"You said there was a snake . . ."

"I myself am unable to recall incident clearly, but the cause of it is unimportant." His eyes focused on something far away, he began to reminisce. "For about a month afterward, nothing but good things happened to me. I made peace with an estranged friend. My parents, usually so chilly to each other that you could almost see their breath, attended a garden party with me and acted like a family. When I made requests of others, they usually agreed, and if they didn't, I was patient and able to explain myself without getting angry. That month was extraordinary."

He paused and swallowed, showing uncharacteristic hesitancy.

"Please don't laugh when I say this, but you are like a goddess of Fortune to me. My Lady Luck."

Karin waved her hands in agitated protest. "Whoa! I mean, that's very flattering, but not me at all!"

How could she be anybody's Lady Luck? She was only a vampire, and a defective one at that.

He paid no heed to her denial. "Would you be willing to embrace me again, like you did three months ago?"

Karin shrunk back into the far corner of her leather seat. She looked from Youichiro to the driver. Was he serious?

Youichiro had been leaning closer, but at her evident panic, he drew back, restoring the gap between them. "I know it may just be coincidence, but I have to find out."

She didn't want to talk about it, but she didn't know how to stop him, since she could hardly jump out of a moving car. "How can you say it like that? We're not alone here!" Just when he'd been acting human, here he was treating his servant like a piece of furniture.

"Nakaoka has been the chauffeur for the Juumonji Group for more than twenty years. He's trained not to listen to conversations in the back seat and not watch what we're doing. He and my butler Sasaki are the people I trust most in all the world. You need pay them no attention."

It might be okay for you, but it bugs the hell out of me! Karin put her head in her hands.

Of course, it wasn't just that she had a problem with embracing him in front of his driver. How could she tell him that she'd done a bit more than just hug him in the park that day? She'd bitten him, driving her fangs into his flesh, pumping her blood into him.

He has such white skin. No blemishes, no moles, no pimples. Such a beautiful neck. His jugular is right there . . .

Oh no! She couldn't allow herself to think this. Her blood had almost settled down, but now it came roaring back. Her heart raced; her body temperature rose.

Oh, crap! My brother may think it's perfectly normal for lovers to bite each other, but we aren't lovers—and besides, the driver is sitting right here—he'll think I'm some kind of kinky freak!

This was all too sudden. Even if she called Anju, her little sister wouldn't get here in time to rescue her. Besides, it wasn't like she could just whip out her cell and start texting.

Argh, what should I do? This is really, really dangerous! It's here!

She hugged herself tightly, keeping her head low, moaning.

"Sorry," whispered Youichiro. "It's too much to ask, hugging someone you don't even love. I can wait until you're ready." His voice lacked its customary arrogance. Sadness flickered like a shadow across his noble features.

Karin's bowed head shook beneath her clasped hands in partial denial. "It's not like I *hate* you or anything."

Sure, the way he didn't listen to people or worry about who might be watching was a little alarming, but he was a fundamentally good person, she felt sure of that. And he looked like the very picture of a prince; what girl in her right mind could be upset when a boy like that said he needed her?

"It's just all so sudden, and I'm not ready to . . ." Karin's voice trailed off, her eyes widening as she realized the hidden meaning behind his words. "Then what you need is only the luck?"

Youichiro's face stiffened, then he looked away. Karin took this to mean she'd hit the nail on the head.

"So that was it," she said as much to herself as to him. "I thought there was something strange. A prince like you would never fall in love with a girl like me."

Her brother and sister were right. Asako and the girls who'd tormented her were right. They were all right. Karin had been racking her brains to figure out why he could possibly want her. Now that the mystery was solved, she felt oddly relieved. Crestfallen, but relieved.

For some reason, she thought of Kenta Usui. Despite all the problems her clumsiness caused for him, he always took her side. He always helped her out. She thought of his wild, wild eyes, of how fierce he looked when he was embarrassed.

Why was everything blurry? Her eyes were wet.

Oh, no, the moment I think of Kenta, I tear up . . .

Karin turned away, blinking furiously.

Youichiro misinterpreted her tears. "Wait! I know I sounded self-centered, but that's not what I meant." He took Karin's hand. "Yes, the reason I had someone looking for you was because I thought you were my Lady Luck. I repeat, *was*. It's much more than that now. You're important to me. I'm sure I can make you happier than anyone else you're likely to meet. Presents, dates, vacations—anything you want is yours. You're cute, and from talking to you I know you're a good girl. I'm not just looking for luck." He was talking pretty fast now, trying to convince himself. He knew perfectly well his motivations weren't purely romantic, which was why he was trying to cover with promises. But his voice was in earnest. He pressed a handkerchief into her hand.

Overwhelmed, Karin forgot to take her hand away. "Even if I do what I did last time, your father might not get better."

"I know all that! I already said it might just be coincidence. But what other options do I have? I tried more than ten girls before I found you. I really do think you're my good luck charm. So, please?"

Holding Karin's hand so tightly it hurt, he twisted his body around so that he could peer directly into her face.

The Blood Injector Has Much to Worry About

What should I do?

Her hand hurt. It was hot. Her face was hot. Her whole body was hot. Her chest was like a drum machine.

Youichiro was so close to her and so good looking, she felt dizzy. His throat was less than a foot from her lips.

If we stay this close, my blood really will get out of control!

But even as she thought this, her head was moving, instinctively bringing her mouth closer to her prey. Her breath was sweet and warm, her heart beating like a hummingbird. It would feel so *good* to just grab him and sink her teeth into him.

I want . . . I want . . . to bite!

Rational thought was slipping away. Nothing registered but her need and the memory of his soft neck and the sweet release of her bite.

Suddenly, the driver slammed on the brakes.

"Aaiiee!" Completely unprepared, Karin was flung against the seat in front of her. She hit her head exactly where it was still tender from the day before. Falling to her knees on the padded floorboard, she rubbed her bump with both hands.

"Are you okay?" asked Youichiro. "Nakaoka, what are you doing?" Unlike Karin, he'd managed to remain upright, having steadied himself against the seat in front of him.

"Sorry, Master Youichiro," mumbled the embarrassed chauffeur. "Some sort of bird just flew right across the windshield. We're in the western district. What now?"

Still holding her head, Karin looked out the window and saw an ancient bus stop sign. They were about as near to her home as a car driven by humans was going get.

"Here is fine! My house is just around the corner!"

"May I drop you at the door?"

"No, thanks; I don't want to make my mother angry."

"Very well, then. Sorry about the sudden stop." The driver stepped out of the car and opened the door for Karin. Youichiro stepped out as well.

"Thank you. I'll give the handkerchief back tomorrow."

"Don't worry about it. More importantly, I truly do need you. And I can take care of you. I really mean that."

Karin silently stared at her toes.

"I won't try to force you. I can wait until you feel ready. Please think about it." Giving her one last nod, he climbed back into the car.

Motor purring, the Benz pulled away from the curb. Youichiro stared at her silently through the tinted glass. Making a U-turn in the empty lot across it the street, the car drove back the way it had come. As it disappeared around one of the neighborhood's many winding curves, Karin let out a big sigh of relief.

I came so close to biting him.

A glance at her watch told her she had to get a move on. She had just enough time to go home, change, and get to work. Dodging puddles on the asphalt road, she strode along quickly, thoughts flittering like bats in her head.

So now I know why Youichiro wants to go out with me. It's a little depressing, but at least it makes sense.

When he said he wasn't looking just for luck, his face and his voice were very serious. But the more serious he looked, the more he seemed to be trying to convince himself as well as her. If he hadn't noticed the streak of luck he'd had after she'd attacked him in the park, and if his father's accident hadn't made him unhappy, he would never have come looking for her.

Sure, I'd like to help him, but I don't think me biting Youichiro is going to make his father recover. My brother says he can't remove the source of his girlfriends' problems, only how they feel.

Sure, her brother Ren had a taste for stressed-out people and when he drank their blood, he also drained away their stress. But the vampiric effect only worked on the immediate victim. Even with the stress removed, the source of it—rush-hour traffic, difficult work, an obnoxious mother-in-law, a domineering boss—remained.

In Karin's case, unhappy people were the ones she wanted to bite. The sadness in them called to her blood, making it surge through her veins and pulsate at the base of her fangs. Youichiro's sorrow spurred her metabolism, her pumping heart, her swelling veins, her most basic need. But although she could assuage that need by biting him, and reduce his immediate sorrow in the process, none of that would wake his father up. Injecting her blood into him would be like medicating him with an antidepressant, and she wasn't sure he needed that.

If he was driven so far into a corner that he had someone look for me, then I do feel sorry for him. Wait. He had someone look for me?

Karin shivered, despite the warm sunlight. She mentally replayed the conversation in the car. Yes, he definitely said: "I had someone looking for you."

He also said that he had "tried more than ten girls" before finding her. But he'd only transferred the previous day. If he'd hugged more girls at her school, then Karin wouldn't have been the focus of all the gossip.

So he'd been looking before he transferred. And he'd been using someone else to do the work for him. So where and how had these girls been "tried"?

She was freezing now. At some point, her fast brisk trot had turned into a run.

The kidnappings in the nature park, they started while I was out of school, two weeks ago. All victims were from my school—Fukumi knew there'd been at least seven. And there were probably more who hadn't said anything. It could easily be more than ten who'd been kidnapped.

Not only kidnapped. Someone had molested them, leaving a hundred thousand yen in their bags. That's, what, a million yen total? How many perverts have that kind of money?

Youichiro did. And so many other things matched up. If Youichiro had ordered someone to kidnap girls for him, that explained everything.

But Youichiro has been such a perfect gentleman with me! He doesn't seem like the kind of person who would drug a girl and do God knows what with her while she's unconscious!

Sure, he'd hugged her without warning yesterday, but that was because he had mistakenly believed her to be in love with him. When she struggled, he immediately let her go.

And when he believed Kenta Usui had assaulted her, his eyes had been like ice, harder and fiercer than Kenta's. That sure didn't seem like acting. If he himself were molesting girls, would he really get so angry about someone else doing it?

But everything else fit.

Ew. I don't know! I just don't know!

She couldn't keep this all in her head. She had to talk to someone.

Karin reached her house, burst through the doors, and rushed inside. Impatiently, she changed her shoes for slippers.

"Mom, I'm home!"

"She's sleeping," said her sister.

"Hey, Anju . . . ouch!" Karin had slammed her face into a scrap of wood sticking off a pillar. She put her hands over her nose and wailed. Every window in the house was covered in thick curtains, making it pitch black inside, so she couldn't see the dangers.

"You know perfectly well Mama and Papa don't wake up before sunset unless there's an emergency."

It appeared Anju had just gotten home from elementary school. She rarely went, but today had been overcast enough for her to make a token appearance. Instead of her usual gothic black dress, she wore a gray mid-length skirt and a white blouse that, while frilly, was still something an ordinary child might wear.

"So it's only you?"

Anju nodded. "Ren didn't come home. Might be out all night again. You're a mess. What happened?"

"Why do you think something happened?" Karin sure felt like a mess, but she didn't like it being so obvious.

"You're beet-red, covered in sweat, and your nose is bleeding."

"It is?" She touched her face. Either because of Youichiro's recent proximity or her collision with the pillar, it sure was. Karin fumbled in her bag for a tissue. "Oh gross, I hope it stops before I get to Julian."

"Should be fine. It's just a normal nosebleed, not your special time of the month. But what's with the handkerchief on your shoulder?"

Karin hesitated, tissue clamped to her nose. She wanted help, but wasn't comfortable broaching the subject of kidnapping and sexual assault with her little sister.

How do I say, "Hey, that boy you wanted me to go for it with may be a perverted rapist!" to someone who's in elementary school? I mean, this is Anju, so she might not even blink, but I'd rather not take the chance.

She would have to talk to her mother when she got back from work.

"When Mama wakes up, tell her I have something I need to talk with her about, so would she please stay home? I've got to change and go to work."

"Okay, but you'd better hurry. It's past four already."

"Crap! Crap, crap, crap, crap!"

Leaving the house without further incident beyond a stumble that didn't quite turn into a fall, she barely managed to get to the family restaurant on time.

Not many people were there yet, but in a little while their rush period would start. She hurriedly changed into her uniform, tripping over her own feet only once. At least her nose had stopped bleeding.

She tied the apron over her blouse and skirt, put on the paper hat, and threw a checkered scarf loosely around her shoulders, fastening it with a scarf ring. She was in too much of a hurry, and got the skirt fastener caught in the fabric and the scarf on backward, but was somehow she was able to redo it and make it out onto the floor on time.

What is that beeping noise?

A familiar voice murmured something that, while too low to hear, was probably a curse. There was Kenta Usui fighting with the cash register. He looked like he wanted to pound it like a boxing champion in a mixed martial arts match.

"Stop beeping at me, damn you!" he growled.

It was the register alarm, growing steadily louder.

Karin ran over to him. "Kenta, here; hit the reset button!"

Their fingers touched it together. The noise stopped.

Letting out a huge sigh of relief, Kenta wiped his brow with the back of his hand. "Sorry. I dropped a coin and went to put it back in, but when I touched the drawer, it suddenly started making that racket."

"When you want to open the drawer, you have to push here. Otherwise the alarm goes off."

Kenta clearly wasn't making friends with this register. The last time he'd pushed the wrong button, receipt paper had gone unfurling across the floor like a party favor.

Perhaps fearing further trouble, Kenta put the coin next to the register rather than into it. He looked at Karin with relief. "Thanks. Don't know what I would have done if you hadn't come."

"No, no, thank *you.*" Karin hung her head. They had parted so badly at school, with her all tongue-tied and unable to explain his innocence to the watching crowd. It was incredible that he was still speaking to her.

"For what?" he asked casually, although he surely had to know.

"For what you did at school." Hmm, that wasn't the best phrase for even a defective vampire to use, but never mind. "I mean, you go and save me and instead of thanking you, I run away like a total spaz. Yeah, I was embarrassed, but I left you looking, like—well, you know. I just totally suck, that's all." Nervous, she looked away.

Kenta scowled in what she knew was embarrassment rather than anger. "Don't worry about it. I don't mind. I mean, *he* pissed me off a bit, but not you."

"I explained everything to Youichiro," said Karin hurriedly, wishing she could spit out her guilt with the words. "He admitted he leaped to the wrong conclusion and even promised to apologize tomorrow."

"Him? Apologize?" Kenta's wild eyes widened.

"He's a little strange and doesn't always listen to people, but he's not a bad person." She felt a small pain in her chest, like the prick of a thorn. *Except maybe he is. Maybe he's worse than Kenta thinks.*

The bad thoughts didn't just flit like bats now; they swarmed in her head like locusts. This was too big to keep to herself.

Kenta immediately noticed that something was wrong. "What is it?"

At that moment, their boss passed by. At the sight of them, a smile spread across his big round face. "Would somebody mind fetching me a case of coasters and a box of kid's dinner set toys from the storage room? Actually, it will probably take both of you."

Their boss seemed to have a thing about sending Karin and Kenta off on errands together.

"Kenta, make sure you carry the heavier box, like a gentleman. Oh, pardon me, ma'am, would you like dessert?" The last was toward a beckoning customer. "Let me bring that to you!" He waddled toward the woman, looking like he might move faster if he just rolled on his side.

On their way to the storage room, Kenta asked Karin what was wrong. "For a moment there, you looked like someone had just kicked you in the stomach. Were you thinking of those stupid girls in the restroom? They'll have moved on to a new target by tomorrow."

"It's not them, Kenta."

"Is it Youichiro, then? Did he try something? He didn't assault you on the way home or anything, did he?"

Now that Kenta had brought up Youichiro Juumonji's name, Karin couldn't hold it in.

She spun toward Kenta, barely restraining herself from throwing her arms around him. "It's not what he did to me, it's what he might have done to others! I don't want to think he could kidnap girls and molest them while they're unconscious!" The mental locust swarm was a buzzing black cloud around her, blurring her vision.

Kenta reached out and gently gripped her shoulders, then drew back as if afraid she might misinterpret the gesture. "What are you talking about? Kidnap who? Molest who? Hey, don't cry, just slow down and tell me about it." Flustered, he pulled some tissues out of his pocket.

She wiped her eyes and blew her nose. "Thank you."

"So what's this got to do with Youichiro? Start at the beginning, okay?"

In the quiet storage room, Karin quickly told Kenta everything.

It's often said that boys and girls live in their own separate worlds. In this case, it seemed to be true. He hadn't heard about the string of kidnappings in the nature park. The girls who experienced it had told other girls, or at least some of them had, and those girls had told still more girls, but not one of them had told a boy.

So Karin had to fill him in about the abductions and then explain how Youichiro had started looking for her at the same time that the kidnappings began, and that the number of girls he claimed to have "tried" was disturbingly similar to the number of victims.

Kenta was understandably shocked, but at first only in a removed kind of way, as when one hears some gossip that may be disturbing but doesn't affect one personally. His reaction became more horrified and when she got to her suspicions about Youichiro Juumonji.

"Hmm. He's got the car and the house, discrete and loyal servants, and all the money he'd need to pull this off," said Kenta, taking a box of paper coasters down from the shelf.

"But . . . but—it just doesn't fit his personality!" protested Karin, searching for the box with the plastic toys in it. "When he thought you'd torn my uniform, he got so angry! Would a pervert do that?"

"Maybe, maybe not. I mean, he did grab you without warning in the middle of the hall. You can't trust guys who

do crap like that." There was a new note of fury in his voice. "My mother has that stuff happen to her at work all the time," he growled, punching a box of paper cups.

Sensing that he'd said more than he'd intended, Karin looked at him in surprise.

Kenta quickly changed the subject. "Anyway, I certainly haven't talked to him as much as you have, so I couldn't say."

"In the hallway, that was a mistake—I mean, he let me go as soon as I started to struggle. And in the car he was a perfect gentleman. He said he would wait 'til I was ready, that he wouldn't try to force me into anything!"

Still holding the box of coasters, Kenta spun around, making a face like he'd just swallowed a cup of vinegar. "Ready? Ready for *what?*"

She hadn't meant to let that slip out. "Erm, nothing much."

"And why was he looking for you in the first place?"

"Well, that's complicated." She couldn't reveal Youichiro's family secrets, especially since she didn't know that he really was involved in the molestations. Plus, she had her own secrets to keep.

"He seems to believe I'm a goddess of Fortune," was the best she could manage. It sounded really silly when she said it.

Kenta gaped, nearly dropping the box of coasters. "You, a goddess? You?"

Was that sound he made a strangled laugh? Karin glared at him silently.

Realizing his faux paux, Kenta hurriedly continued. "Sorry, that's not what I meant. It's just that Youichiro clearly doesn't know you very well."

That did not improve matters.

Despite yet another blow to her ego, she took his point. A high school girl who tripped and flashed her panties all the time could hardly be considered a goddess.

"Anyway, I don't *think* Youichiro is the kidnapper. But the details match up too well, so I'm kind of worried just the same." She finally found the toy box half-buried on the bottom shelf. Pulling it out, she hefted it with a grunt. "Maybe I should ask him directly."

"No, that's too dangerous!" yelled Kenta.

She turned around to find him flushed red, eyebrows raised like warning flags, coupled with the most serious scowl she'd seen yet.

"I mean, what if he *is* guilty? If he knows you suspect him, he might panic. On TV shows, guys like that always try to silence witnesses. Please don't say anything to him."

"But Kenta, Youichiro would never do anything like that!" Her words sounded unconvincing even to her. Even though it had been over three months since their encounter in the park, she'd only known him for one day, and she'd just learned about his family history a couple of hours ago. How could she really know? How could she say anything about him for sure? He'd already revealed one unsuspected side to his personality, albeit a benign one. What face might she see if she blurted out her suspicions?

"So what should I do?" she murmured as she left the storage shed, the box in her arms.

Kenta's only immediate response was a sigh. Not exactly helpful.

She couldn't go to the police with nothing more than a vague suspicion, especially not when the person she suspected was the heir to such a powerful family. If she was right, he'd attempt to silence her the first chance he got. If she was wrong, she'd have humiliated someone who'd been kind to her. Yet it was also too dangerous to talk to him directly . . .

"Well, we can't talk about it here," said Kenta when they reached the floor. "After work?"

"Yeah, thanks." Maybe he'd have some useful suggestions by then, because she sure wasn't coming up with anything.

"Report," said the man, putting down his baccarat glass. The sun hung low in the western sky; its rays, refracted by the whiskey, gave the glass a coaster of golden light on the mahogany table. Both the whiskey and the glass containing it were of the highest quality. So was everything else in the room, except for the middle-aged man in the leather easy chair, his gut spreading out from beneath his dirty tee shirt.

Standing at attention, Sasaki bowed his head. "Nakaoka sends word that Master Youichiro has made a change in his schedule and is planning to swing by the hospital."

The large man laughed. " 'Master' Youichiro? We hardly need to use his honorific here." The bitterness in his eyes belied his mirth.

Sasaki bowed low. "A mere habit, sir."

"Yes, yes," said the large man impatiently. "So, filled with filial piety, Youichiro has gone to see his dear father. Seems like a waste of time, since the old man's just going to sleep through the visit."

"If he follows his usual custom, after the visit he'll make the car wait while he takes a walk. Alone. In the large park located conveniently near the hospital."

"Stupid brat. If he knows it's going to depress him, why does he even bother visiting? It's not like his father is going to care. Still, we can profit from his masochism."

"Sir?"

The man shifted his girth. Beneath him, the sturdy Italian-made easy chair groaned like a ship at sea.

"It's our chance to put the finishing touches on this serial kidnapping and sexual assault case. He has no alibi tonight. Was he really wandering gloomily in the park, thinking about his incurable father, or was he merely stalking his next victim?"

"So we should kidnap someone again?"

The big man snorted like a horse. "Not this time. You say our young master thinks he's found his Lady Luck?"

Sasaki nodded. "A mere freshman at Shiihaba High School. Karin Maaka."

The big man stroked his chins. "A spoiled little rich kid, used to getting everything he wants, all hot and bothered about a common public school freshman. What might a boy like that do if she rejected him? I think he might assault her. Even kill her." He licked his wide lips before taking another sip of whiskey.

Sasaki frowned but said nothing.

"We thought one of the girls would surely go to the police," continued the big man. "Once there was an investigation, it would be child's play to plant a few clues or drop a few anonymous tips to draw attention Youichiro's way. But there hasn't been an investigation, because the silly cows didn't want a fuss. Time to raise the stakes."

Sasaki finally spoke. "Surely there are ways to do that without committing murder."

The large man ignored him. "That should really do quite nicely. When it's all over the news that a girl's been killed, one of the previous victims will panic, thinking how easily it could have been her, and contact the authorities. Then we've won. After all, it was Youichiro Juumonji who ordered the kidnappings. He'll be arrested as a serial rapist. And of course for the murder!" The man laughed so hard his body shook in seismic waves, his face flushed like a drunkard's. But it was his idea, not the whiskey, that intoxicated him.

Sasaki clearly had some misgivings. "Isn't murder going a bit far?"

Another snort. "What, now you're scared? Don't be such an old woman. You've already betrayed Youichiro. You won't get your reward until he's arrested. Besides, you've been his accomplice in the kidnappings. Who do you think will take the fall for that, if not him?"

Sasaki hung his head. "I understand that, yes."

"Good. Now let's not lose our big chance. The brat has no alibi! Grab Karin what's-her-face, kidnap her, snuff her, and dump her in the park. Drop a few hairs from Youichiro's brush on the body and it's perfect."

Sasaki straightened his eye and looked the other man in the eye. "I'm sorry, sir, but I really must refuse. There are some things I can't be part of, no matter how dirty my hands already are."

Sasaki's reservations were there from the beginning, but the offer had been too tempting. Chairman Masaharu Juumonji showed no signs of waking from his coma. Youichiro, still in high school, was too young to take over. Sasaki wasn't getting any younger. Remaining loyal to the Juumonji family in the naive hope of being cared for in his dotage was all too likely to lead to poverty. The lure of a bundle of quick cash to retire on had proved too strong.

But choosing to temporarily serve this man didn't mean that Sasaki trusted him. He took a step backward, shaking his head.

"I can bring her here. And . . . and I can drop the body off in the park afterward. But no more than that."

The big man snorted yet again. "Coward." But then he sighed in assent. "No matter. There's something to be said for doing this like all the others. If you bring her here first, it will help tie the crime to the kidnappings. So go get her."

"Today? But what about the park tonight? That's when Youichiro won't have an alibi."

"We need to go ahead and get this over with. If he gets a chance to talk about the kidnappings with her, we'll be up the creek."

This was a man who acted on impulse rather than careful deliberation. He latched onto ideas like a terrier with a chew toy. And Sasaki himself wanted it over and done with. After a moment's consideration, he nodded in agreement.

The big man finished the whiskey, licked his lips, and laughed. "Hell, if she really *is* a goddess of Fortune, she's wasted on a punk like Youichiro. Anyway, this may be my last chance to sample a high school girl."

Loathing hidden behind an impassive mask, the butler bowed to the fat man. "Then I shall bring her here. To avoid being seen, it may be as late as nine."

The moment he'd heard the name from Youichiro, Sasaki had found out everything he could about Karin Maaka. He'd only had one to day to investigate, but he already knew her address, phone number, and place of employment. And he was sure she was working that night.

Even with July's late sunsets, it was very dark by eight thirty. Karin and Kenta Usui walked together under the streetlights that lined the road. Their conversation was less than lively.

"You really think it's him?" asked Kenta.

"Yes. No. I don't know. God, what should I do when I see him tomorrow?"

He shrugged. "Try to act normal, I guess."

"I don't even know what normal is anymore."

Both sighed. Neither had been able to come up with a cunning plan, the way that characters in a manga or TV show would have.

They turned off the street lined with houses and apartments, heading into the western district where they both lived. The road wound upward through an urban wasteland of empty lots and half-constructed homes.

It was very quiet. They'd left the bustling crowds behind with the shopping centers. Every now and then the headlights of a passing car would sweep over them, but beyond that they were as alone as they would have been in a forest or graveyard.

"I live this way," Karin said, pointing down a side street.

"Oh, okay." He looked like he wanted to follow her. "Be careful."

"Good night. Thanks again for listening to me vent." Waving, she walked away from him into the darkness.

He called after her, "Karin?"

She turned around. In the harsh light of the street lamp, his eyes looked wilder than ever, but she knew there was softness behind them. "Yes, Kenta?"

He hesitated, slumping as if not sure it was his place to speak. But then he straightened up and spoke clearly, "If there's anything I can do, I will. Just tell me what to do."

Karin blinked away sudden tears. "Oh, Kenta, just . . . you know, do what you always do."

Her heart seemed to pause for a moment before restarting at double speed. It was so loud, she feared he could hear it where he stood. Her body tingled—was there electricity in the air? No, it was her; just her. She'd told Kenta to just do what he always did and now her body was doing what it always did when she thought too hard about him, when he was too close, when that time came again. *No, dammit!*

No point in trying to text Anju; she had to get away from Kenta and she had to do it *now*.

"Th-th-thanks, but have I have to go now—see you tomorrow!" With that, she spun around and ran into the dark. Kenta called after her, but she paid no attention. If she lingered even a moment more, she might give into the urge and bite him.

By the time she reached the top of the hill, she was out of breath. Her legs shook as she leaned against a street lamp.

Suddenly, she realized that she didn't have to trot to keep up with Kenta as they'd walked home. He was well over a head taller than her, with much longer legs, but he'd matched his stride to hers. She felt a glow inside her chest, then something much hotter. Her heart throbbed.

Ack, I was too close to him! My blood's about to overflow . . .

Her body shook. Her heart was a steam furnace, sending superheated blood through her veins—and it was ready to boil over.

Hell, maybe I should have just bitten him! But Anju won't get here in time to erase his memories, and—and then there was what he said.

"If there's anything I can do, I will," she repeated.

She felt as if she'd been trying to balance on rickety stilts ever since realizing Youichiro might be involved in the kidnappings. Kenta's words and the concern on his fierce face had been like a helping hand, reaching up to support her.

THE BLOOD INJECTOR HAS MUCH TO WORRY ABOUT

I can't bite him and inject him with my blood, not after all he's done. Besides, I'd have to put my arms around him to bite him. It's not so embarrassing doing that with strangers, but this is Kenta!

Thinking about putting her arms around him was a mistake. She was white hot now. The hair on her body was tingling; sweat was pouring down her bare legs. She shook her head in an attempt to clear it, but that made her feel like her brain was sloshing around in the pool of blood collecting there.

So hot; so dizzy. Please, I've got to find somebody soon!

Approaching headlights framed her from behind. There was no guardrail, only a white line on the asphalt separating the driving lane from the walking zone. She moved as close to the edge as she could.

A white Japanese-made sedan passed by her, slowing to a stop two yards away. Before she could even wonder what was up, the driver leapt out, his face hidden under a dark ski mask. Shrieking, Karin turned to run. It never occurred to her that she could bite him. It was another one of those normal human reactions that made her family think she was such a freak.

She made it less than ten paces before her feet slipped in a puddle. As she toppled forward, strong arms wrapped around her, holding her fast.

"No! Let go! Let go of me!"

But the man was much larger than Karin, and his grip was very strong.

"Help me, somebody, help!"

Pulling her close, the man clamped a handkerchief over her face. It was wet and smelled sickeningly sweet, like medicine.

Karin shook her head, calling through the damp fabric, "Help me, Kenta, help!"

Her nose stung. She felt dizzy. Her body temperature was vaporizing the anesthetic; her gasps were drawing it into her lungs. She couldn't feel her kicking feet, her thrashing legs, her flailing arms. Everything was getting dark. She rushed toward the darkness, sinking in it, going out like a match dropped in water.

THE BLOOD INJECTOR IS IN VERY BIG TROUBLE

Kenta Usui stopped in his tracks. He could swear he'd heard a scream in the distance—from the direction that Karin had run.

It had been so faint, it might have just been his imagination. But with the kidnappings and Karin's suspicions about Youichiro, it wasn't like he could take a chance. Kenta was already running by the time he'd finished thinking that.

He heard another scream.

"No! Let go! Let go of me!"

It was faint, but unmistakably her voice.

"Karin!" yelled Kenta, long legs pounding the rising pavement.

The next scream was louder and closer. "Help me, somebody, help!"

His speed increased despite the steepness of the hill. Where was she?

"Help me, Kenta, help!"

The last "help" had been fainter, yet closer, too. He saw a white car and two figures struggling next to it. One was a tall man in a ski mask, the other a small girl in a pale dress and a thin summer cardigan.

"Karin!" Kenta ran faster, but he was too far away.

The man hoisted Karin up and tossed her into the car like a sack of laundry. Kenta was barely halfway up the hill, but the man was already climbing into the driver's seat.

He could hear the car's engine now; it had been idling all this time. He put everything he had into running, every muscle, every thought, every breath. His arms reached for Karin as if he could pull himself through the distance like it was the liquid air of dreams. He knew he was wasting energy, but couldn't help it.

The door closed. The engine revved as the car pulled away from the curb.

"Wait, you bastard!" Kenta screamed, pushing himself onward in a futile attempt to chase the car. The puff of smoke from the exhaust pipe mocked him as the car sped away into the night, tires grinding the bumpy asphalt.

"No!" He gasped, lurching to a halt with his hands on his knees, trying to catch his breath.

What was the make of the car? He hadn't had time to tell; it had been so generic. He'd glimpsed the license plate, but it appeared to be covered in mud. He was too poor to own a cell phone and there were no residences in sight, just warehouses, broken storefronts, and empty lots.

Back down the hill there was a pay phone. He turned and ran back the way he'd come, cursing himself for not walking Karin home.

He had to think; had to recall everything he'd just seen.

Karin had been limp when the man threw her into the car. There'd been a white cloth in his hand. He remembered what she'd told him about the kidnappings, how the girls had been drugged.

The man had been wearing a suit. His face was hidden by the ski mask, but his body language wasn't that of a young man. This wasn't just some passing thug, grabbing a random girl off the street. It must have been planned.

Youichiro sent someone to snatch Karin.

If that was the case, he had an awful idea what was going to happen next.

This is bad . . . Really, really bad. I've got to save her!

He could go to the cops, but what evidence did he have? They wouldn't even be able to check the Juumonji estate, not on the word of a poor high school student who was probably just jealous of a wealthy heir. They'd say he was making it all up. His testimony might be considered later, if she was missing for over a day, or if they found . . .

He didn't want to think about what they might find later. The point was that they wouldn't believe him until it was too late to prevent anything. For Karin's sake, he had to get moving. Whatever it was he did, he'd have to do it himself, and he'd have to do it now.

Where did Youichiro say his house was? Ootani and Kida had been talking about how they wanted to drop in on him sometime. As he ran, Kenta tried to remember that scrap of overheard gossip.

Yeah, near the Amamiya Catholic Church! That was it; that's where he lives!

He saw a phone booth up ahead, but ran past it.

There was a bus stop across the street. The bus went straight to the church district. It would only take half an hour. Much faster than he'd ever get the cops to listen to him. He knew where the big church was, so he should be able to find Youichiro's home. *Please let me be in time. If you've hurt her, you sick bastard, I'll kill you!*

Hang on, Karin!

It didn't occur to him how much faster a taxi would have been until he got off the bus. Kenta was a poor boy from a single-parent household. Taxis were just something he saw on TV. He probably wouldn't have been able to afford the fare, anyway.

Now, where the hell was Youichiro's house?

An old man sweeping the front steps of the church informed him that the area was known as the Estate Quarters. Every estate was large enough to hold ten apartment buildings like the one Kenta lived in. The old man didn't know the Juumonji estate and there was no one else to ask for directions beneath the elaborately decorated streetlights. Nobody *walked* anywhere in upscale neighborhoods like this.

Kenta raced from house to house, checking the names on each. Every house was surrounded by a long, tall fence of some sort, so it was difficult to even find the gates much less the nameplates.

"Damn, damn, damn, damn!" gasped Kenta, running beside an ivy-covered brick wall. He could see a wrought-iron gate up ahead. When he reached it, he found a brass plate engraved with the name "Juumonji" set above the intercom.

At last! But wait—is this really somebody's house?

He stared through the gates the building beyond. From the terrifyingly long wall, he'd expected a large mansion. Every damn estate in the district was large. But this . . . this was huge! The gate alone was the size of those at school, but their school could never have afforded the iron scrollwork, elegantly molded into the shape of vines.

Pressing his face against that cold decoration, Kenta peered inside.

It was still night, of course, and the spreading trees in the garden blocked much of his view. Where was the house? The grounds were too big. Whatever happened in there, nobody on the outside would hear.

Kenta pressed the intercom button. After a moment, a haughty woman's voice asked, "Who is it?"

"My name is Kenta Usui. I go to Youichiro's school."

"Ginrei Academy?"

"No, Shiihaba High School."

"Oh. I'm not aware of any appointment." Even over the intercom, he could hear the change in the tone of the woman's voice. Clearly he wasn't welcome here.

Screw that. "It's important!" he snapped. "Please let me in; I have to see him!"

"Master Youichiro has not yet returned."

"Liar!" he yelled. She hadn't claimed her master wasn't at home until she heard the name of Kenta's school. Surely she was hiding something.

"Open the door and let me in!" He shook the door in the gate, but the sturdy iron didn't budge.

"Stop that at once! I don't wish to call the police on one of Master Youichiro's classmates, but I will! Go away."

"I've done nothing to be arrested for—I just want to see Youichiro."

"Then stop shaking the gates. That's the action of a thug, not a friend."

She must be watching him on a monitor. Taking a step back, he looked for the security camera.

"Go home," she said coldly. "I shall inform Master Youichiro of your visit." The intercom clicked off.

He started to press the button again, but then thought better of it. The same servant would answer, so it was clearly pointless. He peered around. Where was that damn camera? There, hidden in the branches above the gate, he caught the dull glint of a lens.

Feigning resignation, he turned and walked away. The second he was around the corner, he started to run. The estate's brick walls were tall and thick, but covered in ivy. Maybe he could climb them.

Fifty yards down the wall, he stopped. *Japan's too small for a house like this,* he thought to himself. Then again, the size of the place might be in his favor. There had to be some blind spots. After making sure nobody was watching, he scrambled up the wall.

It was harder than he'd expected. The gaps between the bricks were very narrow. He had to really jam his fingers and toes into them to get a grip. The first three times he tried, he slid back down, scraping his fingers painfully on the bricks.

Gritting his teeth, he tried again. This time he made it well above his own height without slipping back down. He was very close to the ivy hanging over the top of the wall. When he reached that, things would be easier.

Suddenly a car turned the corner, catching him in its headlights like a convict making a prison break.

Kenta froze. It was too late to jump down and pretend to be a pedestrian. He was clearly and obviously in the midst of breaking and entering. "Don't notice me," he prayed, clinging to the wall like a cockroach. "Drive on by and don't notice me."

So much for prayers. The car stopped right next to him. It was a silver-white Benz.

The rear window opened and he heard a familiar chilly voice. "Don't climb any higher, Kenta. There are motion detectors and security cameras on top. Or is it your intention to set off an alarm?"

"Youichiro!" Kenta yelped, sliding painfully back to the ground. But if he really hadn't been home, who'd kidnapped Karin?

"Ouch!" Kenta had landed on his rear at the base of the wall. Looking up, he saw Youichiro open the car door. From the open window, he could hear the driver's worried voice.

"Stay inside while I call the police, Master Youichiro. This boy was clearly trying to climb the wall."

"That won't be necessary. I know him. He's no threat to me."

Youichiro walked to him and, to his great surprise, helped him to his feet. "I'm sorry about the misunderstanding at school," he said, brushing off the astonished Kenta. "I leapt to a very unfortunate conclusion." There was no mockery in his tone, just an honest apology.

Kenta had no idea how to react.

Maybe Karin had been right to think Youichiro couldn't do something like this, but she *had* actually been kidnapped. Which meant . . .

Kenta grabbed the front of Youichiro's shirt. "Is she in there? Did you have her kidnapped? Tell me, you bastard!"

Youichiro might be two years older than him and much richer, but he didn't care. There was no time for being polite. The kidnapping could still have been carried out at his command, with Karin held inside his mansion until he returned. Thinking of that, Kenta pulled back his right hand, making a fist.

Youichiro didn't flinch, didn't shove him away, or make any move to defend himself. Something like guilt flashed across his face.

Kenta held back on hitting him, preferring a verbal attack for now. "It had to be you; the timing matches up too well. What are you planning to do to Karin, you pervert?"

"I'm not planning to do anything with her. I've not even seen her since I dropped her off near her home."

"Liar! You've got her hidden in your house!"

"Who are you calling a liar?" snapped Youichiro, knocking Kenta's hand aside. "Are you having delusions of Karin being held captive inside my house? Is that why you tried to climb my wall? Well, come on inside with me and I'll show you just how crazy you are." Walking back to the car, he opened the door and glared at Kenta. "Well? I'm calling your bluff, so get in!"

Nonplussed at Youichiro's confident scorn, but also both frantic to get to the bottom of the mystery and too

stubborn to back down, Kenta obeyed. Only after Youichiro slid in beside him did it occur to Kenta that the older boy might have something planned for him inside. *Just let him try it,* he thought, anger making him feel invincible.

The Benz started moving. They sat side by side in strained silence. When the car reached the impressive gates, the driver clicked a remote to silently open them.

Rich people! thought Kenta with disdain and envy.

The car drove on through the shadowed garden. A few dozen yards on, the headlights picked up a second lower wall and another, plainer gate. Beyond that was a three-story Western-style mansion. Kenta was secretly glad that his attempt at sneaking in had been foiled. The place was so big, like a combination of a park and a museum—he would have been completely lost.

Youichiro's arrival had apparently been expected, for the front door opened at their approach. A middle-aged woman in a dark-colored frock and apron bowed, then stepped aside to let them pass. "Welcome home, Master Youichiro. You must be very tired. How is your father? Ah, I see that your . . . friend . . . is with you." Kenta recognized her voice as that of the servant who'd threatened to call the cops on him, but she sounded much warmer now.

"He's just an acquaintance and won't be needing any tea. Come, follow me." Youichiro beckoned to him with one finger. "You can keep your shoes on."

Despite everything on his mind, Kenta was unable to prevent himself from gawking a little bit. The entrance hall alone was astonishing, more like the lobby of some world famous hotel he'd seen in a magazine than part of someone's home. It was lined with ornate Chinese-looking vases so big he could have hidden in them, and enormous oil paintings of glowering people he presumed were Youichiro's ancestors covered the walls.

The ceiling chandelier was like something out of a big-budget movie, yet this was just the outer foyer. The temperature was perfect, neither too hot nor too cold, and Kenta idly wondered what the electricity bills were like.

Ahead of him, Youichiro opened a polished oak door. Stepping through it, Kenta honestly couldn't decide whether he'd just entered a parlor or a ballroom.

There were clusters of comfortable but very expensive-looking furniture arranged about the open space, like in the reading room of a particularly well-funded public library.

Youichiro sat down on a leather-covered sofa nearest the door.

"Don't just stand there. Sit down. Or would you like to look for Karin first? I'm telling you I've not seen her since I dropped her off this afternoon, but if you don't believe me, feel free to search my home. Or better yet, call her. There's a phone over there." He pointed to an antique phone on a little table near the wall.

The particular combination of annoyance and bemusement in his tone was oddly convincing. "You really dropped her off?"

"I said I did! Go ahead, use the phone!"

Kenta didn't want to admit that he didn't know Karin's number. *Where to begin searching?*

Youichiro wasn't letting him off that easy. "Okay, it's my turn to ask some questions."

"Fine," muttered Kenta. "I'm not the one with anything to hide." Sitting down would give him a chance to consider his options. He chose the sofa opposite Youichiro, not wanting to sit beside the other boy. It gave him a view of both the outer and inner hallways, in case any lackeys should try to take him unawares. Of course, a room this big surely had other doorways even if they weren't immediately apparent, but at least the floor was hardwood (albeit decorated with fancy throw rugs) rather than the deep carpeting he might have expected. He stood a good chance of hearing anyone sneaking up behind him, especially since this was the kind of place where the help were likely to be wearing dress shoes.

"Other than congenital insanity, what makes you think I've kidnapped Karin?"

He looked at Youichiro coldly. "She already suspected you might have something to do with the kidnappings and sexual assaults in the nature park. She didn't like thinking that—she also somehow thinks you're a really nice guy—but there's evidence pointing your way."

Crap, I sound like an idiot trying to imitate a TV show detective.

"I ordered the kidnappings, yes. But there was no need to do it anymore after I found Karin."

Kenta could only gape at the blatant admission. Here he'd been mocking himself for coming off like a TV detective; was Youichiro now going to pull out a gun and sneer like some cool, sophisticated villain?

Except Youichiro wasn't sneering; his tone was cool but utterly matter-of-fact. "And calling it sexual assault is a gross exaggeration. Yes, I had the girls brought here.

Yes, that was an extreme measure. But I could tell each and every one of them was the wrong girl the moment I embraced her, so I immediately sent each one home. No doubt it was frightening for them, but none of them were harmed or molested in any way, and they each ended up with quite a bit of money, at least by their standards."

Kenta wanted to knock that unashamed look off Youichiro's face. "You lying bastard! All the girls are talking about it. Someone removed their clothing while they were asleep. They were molested, maybe raped."

"Be serious. I would never do something that vile."

"Yeah, right. You admitted to kidnapping them."

Youichiro sighed with theatrical impatience. "To having them kidnapped, but that's not the point. I told you, I was looking for Karin. I'd been doing it ever since she embraced me in the park. For the entire month after she did that, everything went unusually well for me. I had to find her and embrace her again; I had to know if she was my Lady Luck."

He paused, then said, "But I couldn't remember anything about her beyond the uniform she wore, so I had someone look out for girls from that school and bring them to me. The only way to test them was to embrace them, but that's all I did."

The sheer improbability of this pissed Kenta off even more. "Why would you, of anyone in the world, need luck?" he snarled.

Youichiro's cold stare was no answer.

"You can't tell me that, yet you expect me to take your word for it that you're not a friggin' pervert?"

Youichiro was the first to blink. Sighing, less in irritation than resignation, he looked past Kenta at the wall. "If you must know, my father's in the hospital."

Big deal, thought Kenta. *This kind of money buys a lot of medicine*. "Surely you can afford the best doctors."

"Yes, of course. The Touto University Hospital's neurosurgery department is the best in the country. But he won't wake up. He's been in a coma for months."

Youichiro slumped in the chair, one hand tightly gripping the armrest, his eyes avoiding Kenta's face.

This vulnerability took Kenta completely aback. "What happened?"

"A car accident. Random, stupid chance. The chairman of the Juumonji Group is personally in charge of a number of enterprises, yet now he's asleep, eating through a tube, getting washed and changed by nurses. I know it's stupid to go chasing after a superstition. But I can't think of anything else to do."

"But kidnapping? Didn't your mother try to stop you?"

"My mother's traveling somewhere. We can't get in touch with her. The news was everywhere, even Europe, but she hasn't called. She must have made up her mind to get divorced. My family is finished." There was a small sound at the back of his throat that just might have been a whimper.

Kenta had no response to this.

"When I first met Karin, my mother and father weren't speaking; I was fighting with a close friend over, well, nothing—hell, I wasn't really getting along with anyone. But after she hugged me, everything changed—everything got better. My friend and I patched things up. I was able to get my parents talking to each other again. Is it so wrong to want that type of good fortune again?

He said that last sentence less like a confident young heir than a frightened little boy. To his great surprise, Kenta found himself sympathizing with Youichiro.

He cares more about his father than I would have expected.

Kenta understood devotion to a parent. He lived alone with his single mother, for whom he'd do just about anything. Empathy softened his tone. "Were you with your father today? Your housekeeper asked you about him."

"No. I tried. I went to the hospital, but I can't stand seeing him like that. There's nothing I can do for him—he's got nurses at all times. I want to be a good son, but I can't deal with him just lying there. So I went to the park beside the hospital. I wanted to be alone. I had to be alone."

"Don't be such an idiot!" Kenta yelled, jumping to his feet.

Sure, Youichiro was genuinely worried about his father, but the way he was dealing with it was so stupid.

"If you've got time to go moping in the park, you've got the time to sit with him. And don't give me any crap about how it pains you to see him like that. He's the one in pain, not you."

Youichiro tensed. "But I can't do anything for him, and it's tearing me apart."

"Talk to him. Hold his hand. I read somewhere that people in comas understand more than we give them credit for. Since you can't get hold of your mother, you're the only one who's there for him." Kenta glared down at the shocked Youichiro, towering over him. "It's too late for regrets! You've got no time to go chasing after luck! That's just escaping from the reality of the situation!"

Youichiro didn't argue, but simply slumped further down in his seat.

"Look, I know this is tough to hear. But maybe the reason you were suddenly able to convince people to do stuff after you met Karin in the park is because something changed in *you*, something that temporarily made you actually *listen* to other people. If you did that more often, you might get better results."

Running out of steam, Kenta suddenly found himself embarrassed by his own lecture. Meanwhile, Youichiro continued his uncharacteristic slumping, which made Kenta feel even less comfortable. To hide his embarrassment, he tried to find something else to yell about.

"Anyway, if you were looking for her, you should have just transferred in the first place. And now that you've found her, what the hell was the point of kidnapping her on the way home from work?"

Youichiro's face quivered. "After work?"

"Yeah, about an hour ago. When did you drop her off at home?"

Rather than answering, Youichiro leapt to his feet and snatched the phone off the side table.

"Who are you calling?" Kenta asked, suddenly worried that Youichiro was going to turn him in for trying to climb the wall.

"Karin's house."

"You know her number?" Youichiro felt a twinge of jealousy.

"The second we knew she was who I was looking for, we checked her number out in the student directory."

Catching the worried look in Youichiro's eyes, Kenta fell silent. After a moment, the call connected.

"Good evening and my apologies for calling at this late hour, but is Karin there? This is her friend Youichiro Juumonji. Not yet, you say? No, thank you, I don't need to leave a message." Youichiro put the phone down.

"You said you dropped her off at home!" Kenta cried.

"That was after school. You've seen her since then."

"So where is she now?" A chill ran down his spine as he realized how much time they'd just wasted.

"Kenta, give me details. What happened?"

"Some guy in a ski mask grabbed her and clamped a handkerchief over her face. He threw her in the back of a white car and drove off before I could catch up to them."

Youichiro bit his lip, his usual mask of confidence completely gone now. "I never ordered Karin kidnapped. So who could it have been?"

"Crap!" yelled Kenta, stomping the floor in frustration. "We should call the police. I didn't report it because I thought you'd ordered it and knew they wouldn't take my word over yours. And I had so little to go on—it was too dark to see what kind of car it was, and the plates were dirty so I couldn't read the number. All I could think to do was come here . . ."

"The license plates?" Youichiro twitched, as if he knew something. "Was it a white car? A Nissan March?"

Kenta thought about it. "Could be, yeah." That might not mean much, however, since that model was probably the most popular car in Japan these days. But it was all they had to go on.

"Sasaki drives a March."

"Who?"

"The butler. He's the one who was kidnapping the girls for me. I told him to cover the license plates in mud so nobody could read them."

"What's he look like?"

"Over sixty, sturdy build, about your height."

"Does he wear a dark suit and a ski mask so his victims can't see his face?"

Instead of answering, Youichiro grabbed the phone again and dialed an inside line. But there was no answer.

"Not in his room." He dialed another number. "It's me. Has Sasaki come back yet? I see. You haven't left the kitchen? No, never mind. I'll call his cell."

"Why didn't you call that first?" snapped Kenta.

"He's old fashioned, always leaving it behind. Dammit!" Youichiro was growing more and more agitated. Clearly, nobody was answering the cell number.

Youichiro put the phone down. "Let's check the garage. If his car's there, he's on the grounds somewhere."

"Where's the garage?"

"Outer garden."

They ran through the parlor, down the hall, and out the door. Just doing that wasted more precious time. Kenta mentally cursed the Juumonji family for owning such a huge estate.

He thought of something. "Could this Sasaki have laid his hands on the girls before he sent them home?"

"No, he's been working here forty years, with no history of anything like that. I can't believe he's a pervert!" Youichiro yelled.

They went through the inner gate and ran along the white stone wall. They could see a low, flat, rectangular concrete building through the trees. Clearly, this was the Juumonji garage.

Youichiro pulled out a remote key. The automatic shutters slid quietly open and the inside lights flicked on. Youichiro looked quickly around. "There!" he snapped, pointing to the white Nissan at the end of the garage.

"That's his? Who drives all these other cars?" In addition to the Benz Youichiro had used, there was a Lincoln, a Jaguar, and a long row of foreign cars Kenta was unable to name.

"You need at least one for each person, of course."

Kenta twitched. "People will hate you if say things like that."

"My father has one car for official business and one for private use. The pearl-green one is my mother's. This tasteless, trashy *thing* is my Uncle Tsuneo's."

"You don't like your uncle?"

"I despise him. He has no talent, no sense of responsibility, and he never takes anything seriously, but he likes to put on airs and take the credit. He's run two companies into the ground, and his wife left him after he beat her. My father's always wiped his butt for him. The scumbag doesn't deserve it."

Kenta was carefully examining the Nissan March.

"Yeah, this is it—it's got to be!" He remembered the shape, and the license plates were still caked with mud. No matter how much Youichiro might trust Sasaki, this was pretty damning evidence. Now, if they could only find the butler, they could save Karin.

Just as Kenta was going to say something to that effect, he heard a faint sound. It was distant, indistinct, but still unmistakably a scream.

"Did you hear that?"

"I heard *some*thing."

The two of them silently moved to the garage door, listening closely.

There it was again, a female voice yelling, "Stop!"

This time, Youichiro clearly heard it, too. "There's a warehouse over there. Filled with junk not worth calling antique. Nobody should be in there at this time of night."

Both of them broke into a run. The gravel shone in the garden lights as their feet kicked it up.

Fifteen minutes earlier at the Maaka home, Calera put the phone down and glared at the clock.

"How strange. Karin should have been finished work ages ago . . . Anju!"

Anju appeared in the door with her doll clutched in her arms. "Yes, Mother?"

"You said Karin had something she wanted to talk about after work?"

"Yes. She's very late now." Anju gazed out the window. "She should have been home an hour ago."

Pale clouds rolled across the blue-black sky, the moon peering through them as though they were strips of torn paper. No stars were visible.

Karin staying out late was as unlikely as Ren coming home early. The only time she'd been this late was when she went on that junior high field trip.

"Should I go see if she's still at work?" Henry asked, fiddling with his mustache.

Calera shook her head. "The bats will be faster."

"Then let me," Anju said, looking through the window. She could control them without the aid of her voice.

Small black shapes suddenly dropped like leathery fruit from the eaves and trees, then spread like umbrellas to catch the wind.

The stillness of the night was broken by hypersonic squeals and the fluttering of many dozen pairs of wings, not that any normal human could have heard either.

"They'll find her in a few minutes."

"You're incredible with those bats," said Calera, looking at her youngest daughter with pride. "I do look forward to your awakening; you'll make a truly splendid vampire." She sighed wistfully. "If only Karin had even half your talent."

Henry put a tentative hand on her shoulder. "At least she does have one vampiric quality . . ."

Before he could finish the sentence, a bat appeared, hanging upside down outside the window, its eyes glinting like tiny black buttons as it twisted its head to look at them.

Anju spun around, her usually calm and confident eyes wide with surprise. "Mama, Karin's in big trouble!"

It was dark. It was very dark.

"Where am I? Is anybody there?"

She tried to open her eyes, but her lids felt so heavy. She was still very sleepy. But she knew she had to wake up. If she didn't, something bad was going to happen.

Suddenly, her arms were yanked upward.

Karin let out a little grunt of pain.

She could hear the noise of fabric rustling, then some sort of cord dug into her wrists. Karin shook her head, struggling. "No, stop, that hurts!"

Her tongue was thick, her legs felt both heavy and boneless and, as for her head, it was as if all the blood that had rushed there earlier had congealed like pudding. She'd never felt this bad in the morning, not even after accidentally taking too much cold medicine.

"She's waking up, isn't she?"

Karin didn't recognize the voice, but it sounded male—and not young.

"Yes, I only gave her one dose. Should I apply it again?" This second voice was also male, both older and less coarse.

"Screw it; she's fine like this, absolutely fine." He lingered on that last word in a way that made her skin crawl.

The man laughed, and it wasn't pleasant. "It's not like she's ever going home again. It's more fun with her awake."

What's happening? Who is this? Karin forced her eyes open, trying to focus. When she did, she screamed.

The first thing she saw was a large, damp, pale face. A thin mouth split in a lecherous grin that reminded her of a Cheshire cat. A pink tongue appeared between the yellow teeth, further moistening the cracked, gray lips.

Blood-shot eyes scanned up and down her body, looking at her in such a slimy way that their gaze practically left slug trails on her skin. The breath that wheezed out of that nasty mouth stank of cigarettes and whiskey.

Karin screamed again. "Get away from me!" She tried to get up and run, but the rope dug into her wrists.

The man backed away a bit, surprised by the scream.

Karin looked around. She saw bare fluorescent bulbs hanging from the concrete ceiling, a dust-covered piano and sofa, a cabinet with broken doors, and more indistinct junk piled nearly to the ceiling.

She was in a storage shed of some kind, but a very large one—as big as the gym at school.

And she was lying on a brass bed with a single bare mattress.

"Ouch! What are you doing?!" she shouted, trying to free her arms, which were pulled up over her head.

"The more you struggle, the more it hurts," said the older and less-coarse voice. "Lie still."

A gray-haired man tied Karin's hands together, then tied that rope to the metal frame of the bed.

She didn't recognize his face, but she knew his sturdy body and dark gray suit. This was the man who'd kidnapped her.

Kidnapped! Just like those other girls. But they were more than just kidnapped.

Once Karin was firmly bound to the bed, the aging man stepped away. The middle-aged man drew near her and again peered into Karin's face.

"Noisy girl. Still, noise is all part of the fun, like a good party. No good at all when they're drugged silent. Oh, no, not at all. Now then, high school girl, let's see how . . . unspoiled you are."

If there'd been any doubt about his intentions, it was gone now.

Karin screamed again. "No! Stop! Let me go! Get away or I'll scream!"

It took her a moment to realize that he was laughing. "But you already have, my pretty!" He cracked his knuckles. "This is fun. I feel like a villain from a samurai movie, but somehow I don't think a hero is going to show up and save you. Scream all you like, nobody can hear you."

"May I go now?" asked the older man, looking extremely uncomfortable.

"What, you're still here? Yes, Sasaki; off with you, so this little girlie and me can have some fun."

Sasaki. Karin thought she'd heard the name somewhere before, but she couldn't remember where.

"When should I return?"

Sasaki's master ran a dirty thumb along Karin's flinching leg, then stuck the digit in his mouth. "An hour," he mumbled, sucking on the thumb. "Give me at least an hour."

Karin screamed wordlessly, her feet kicking against the mattress.

"Come on now," said her tormentor, unfastening his belt. "Let's have more variety than that. Don't just scream; shout 'oh, no!' and 'please don't, please don't!' Then I can say, 'You know you want it.' Too bad you aren't wearing a kimono, so I can't spin you like a top. How's this?"

The man's hands had reached out for her summer cardigan. It had no buttons, but it was bound by a single string. His sausage-like fingers grabbed the string and slowly began to loosen it.

"No, stop! Don't touch me, you dirty freak!"

Since her hands were tied to the bed frame, she couldn't sit up, but she thrashed her legs wildly. Her right foot hooked up and around, and—with what was either blind luck or instinctive accuracy—caught him right on the temple with her heel.

Grunting, the man fell backward off the bed. There was a dull thump as he hit his head again, whether on the floor itself or another object lying there, she couldn't see.

Sasaki paused in the doorway, then turned back into the room. He didn't try to help the man on the floor, just checked to make sure that Karin's bonds were still tight.

"Are you all right, Master Tsuneo?"

"Are you still here? Don't just stand there staring, help me hold her down."

"I was under the impression you wished to see the reactions of an unspoiled high school girl."

"I didn't think . . . she'd fight . . . this much!" panted Tsuneo, picking himself and looking vexed. He rubbed his balding head, which still bore the imprint of Karin's a foot and a nasty bruise. "You know, it doesn't even make sense. I mean, look at her. Sure, she's no dog, but no teen beauty queen either. Just an ordinary high school girl—there must be millions like her."

Even though she knew it was ridiculous, Karin found herself annoyed at being dismissed this way. If this man didn't think she was special, why had he kidnapped her? The next thing she heard left her so astonished, she temporarily forgot to be scared.

"Does that idiot Youichiro really think this bitch is a goddess of Fortune?"

"Youichiro? You mean Youichiro Juumonji? Who are you? How do you know he thinks I'm his Lady Luck?" she asked rapidly.

Tsuneo curled his blubbery lips. "The punk's my nephew, not that it's going to make any difference to you."

So this was the uncle Youichiro has spoken so venomously about. Now she remembered where she'd heard Sasaki's name. She turned to look at the older man. "Then you're Youichiro's butler! How can you do this, with the trust he's put in you?"

"Oh? Sasaki, it seems she's heard of you."

Sasaki sighed. "Master Youichiro is a bit naive. Ten or even five years from now, things might be different. But for now, he is hardly capable of taking over the Juumonji Group from his father. I switched allegiance to Master

Tsuneo in return for enough money to retire early. Master Youichiro is an intelligent boy, but he knows far too little of the world."

Tsuneo looked angry. "Intelligent, my ass. He's a spoiled little rich kid who spends too much of his time with nonsense like this Lady Luck business."

"Certainly, sir," Sasaki said, agreeing readily. He turned back to Karin. "Miss Maaka, isn't it? I regret it had to come to this, but it can't be helped now. I suppose it's even partially my fault.

"When Master Youichiro first wanted to search for you, I warned him of the dangers of involving himself with the general public, and where unscrupulous people can take advantage of him and damage the family name. It was best, I told him, to discretely abduct high school girls walking through the park, in the hope of finding you."

"So he *was* involved in the kidnappings?" Her suspicions had been correct, not that this made her happy.

"Involved? Oh, yes, he was!" Tsuneo laughed, stubbly cheeks jiggling. "The little twit fell right for the plan, never suspecting he was setting himself up as a kidnapper and serial molester!"

It seemed Tsuneo hated his nephew as much as Youichiro hated him. "Youichiro thinks the girls all got home untouched, but I had my fun with them first. Everybody needs some fun!"

Obviously, Tsuneo must have molested the girls while they were still fully under the influence of the drug, whereas Youichiro had hugged them while they were slowly regaining consciousness from the first dose. "You bastard!"

"Yeah, it was a pretty good plan. But the stupid cows wouldn't cooperate by going to the police. He should have been arrested ages ago."

Karin's flash of outrage at what they were planning to do to Youichiro was overwhelmed by what they intended for her. "That's why you kidnapped me—so you could pin something worse on him!"

Tsuneo swelled up a like a pigeon. "Not as dumb as you look, are you? That's right. He'll be the obvious suspect when your body is found, especially when we leave some identifying trinket of his near it. When that happens, some of the girls will surely come forward, too. Even if he's not convicted, the scandal will be the end of him, and the family fortune will finally pass to me. My damn brother's been in a coma for two months; he's never going to wake up. So why haven't they made me chairman already? There's even been talk of Youichiro becoming the provisional chairman—I ask you, is that fair? A high school brat instead of me? If the board had shown any sense and decency, it wouldn't have come to this!"

His frown turned into a grin, and this time he looked like a shark.

"Oh yes, the police will surely be paying the young master a visit this time. A spoiled rich kid like him, dumped by a girl? Not at all surprising if he strangles her, is it?"

Karin shut her eyes at the horror and outrage of what they intended to do, not just to her but to Youichiro, who'd never sought anything but to make his father better. When she opened her eyes again, they were wet. "Poor Youichiro," she whispered.

"She's finally crying!" said Tsuneo happily. He poked her gently in the cheek, then licked the tear from his fingertip. Karin let out a little shriek and pulled her face away.

"It's so sad, I almost want to tell the punk that his girlfriend wasn't worried about herself at all, but cried tears of pity for him."

Karin was plenty worried about herself, but being upset for Youichiro's sake had given her a temporary excuse not to think about that. This was far worse than what had happened to the other girls. It would be fatal.

Desperately stalling for time, she played dumb. "But why haven't you drugged me again? The other girls were all drugged. If you're going to molest me, do it, but I'd rather not have to look at you while it's happening, and I sure don't want to remember it afterward."

Tsuneo looked at her in astonishment. "You think there's going to be an afterward? You can't be that stupid. I know Youichiro called you his Lady Luck and people refer to 'dumb luck' all the time, but that's not just dumb, that's retarded!"

Good; anything that kept him talking rather than *doing* was good.

"I-I-I can't help it if I'm not smart like you. Go ahead, explain it to me."

He giggled. "One would think you were an elementary school student, you're so thick. Maybe you need visual aids?" Making a circle with the thumb and index finger of his left hand, he stuck the index finger of his right one through it in a familiar, obscene gesture. Then he put both hands together in front of him and mimed clasping them around a throat.

She knew it already, of course, but the shock in her voice wasn't feigned. "You're going to . . . kill and rape me?"

"Not in that order; I'm no pervert. Feel free to start screaming now."

She looked toward Sasaki, who was still standing against the wall as if he'd been nailed there. "Please help me!" she said to him. "Don't let him do this. If he does, you're just as guilty."

There was a sudden explosive shock on the left side of her face, blurring her vision. Her cheekbone felt hot. She couldn't keep her eyes open. It took her a few seconds to realize she'd been hit.

"Don't talk to him, talk to me. I'm the master here."

His hands snaked out, grabbing both her ankles before she cold kick him again. With surprising speed for his bulk, he heaved himself on the bed, squatting on her feet. Safe from being struck in the head, he turned and glared at the man behind him.

"All right, Sasaki, even if you're the kind of pervert who likes to watch, I'm just a normal guy who likes his privacy. Come back in an hour and clean up the mess."

"As you wish," said Sasaki, a note of slight distaste in his voice. Karin heard his footsteps retreat. He was leaving her at this foul creature's nonexistent mercy.

Could two human beings really be that monstrous? Could this really be happening? She screamed again.

He slapped her a second time, then giggled. "Yes, I know I said you could start screaming now, but I never said

I wouldn't hit you for it. Don't look so shocked. Surely you don't expect me to be nice about this, do you? I've got an hour to be as naughty as I want, and I'm a very naughty man."

No! Not like this! She thought of her parents, her sister, her brother, even Kenta Usui. *Oh, Kenta, if I was a normal girl living in a normal house, you could have walked me all the way home.*

BA-DUMP. Her heart raced into overdrive. The side of her face where she'd been hit was burning hot, and that heat spread through her body. Despite Tsuneo's great weight pressing down on her feet, her legs shook like she was having an epileptic fit, and the movement traveled through his whole body, causing his double chin and blubbery cheeks to vibrate like jelly.

"What the hell is wrong with you?"

She couldn't have answered even if she wanted to, but she knew what was happening. It could only be one thing.

Her blood rush had been activated. But it couldn't be because of Tsuneo. The man holding her down seemed sadistically happy, with no trace of the sadness that typically caused her veins to boil over.

However, her emotional state had been pushed to its limits since regaining consciousness, and she'd been trying to suppress the urge only moments before she'd been kidnapped and dosed with the chloroform that temporarily shut down the process. Now, stress had reawakened that delayed biochemical reaction, and it was stronger than ever.

Although Tsuneo's face was very close to hers now, it seemed far away, like she was looking at his grotesque features through the wrong end of a telescope . . . through a red filter. Everything was red, so red.

His mouth was moving, saying something gross about how sexy she looked, all red and sweaty and panicky. She could barely hear him over the pounding of her own heart—a steam pipe hammering in her veins, a rushing roar in her head. She was going to blow.

And then she did.

THE BLOOD INJECTOR IS
A GODDESS OF FORTUNE

Why is your garden so damn big?!" panted Kenta. "Who needs this much space?"

There were so many trees, it looked like the thickest part of the Shiihaba Nature Park. There was even a gravel trail—Kenta wondered who needed a *trail* in their yard. He'd been following Youichiro down that twisting past for over a minute now, with no warehouse in site. "Do you have to have so many trees?"

"I like trees," said Youichiro calmly. The bastard didn't even sound out of breath. Weren't rich boys supposed to be pampered and weak?

"Where the hell is this place?"

"There—see the roof up ahead?"

There was a dark, square shape above the trees, but before Kenta got more than a glimpse of it, his attention was distracted by the man who'd appeared on the path ahead of them, moving silently despite the gravel.

Lights from the warehouse shown through the branches, framing his familiar silhouette. Recognizing the shape of the man who'd abducted Karin, Kenta leapt forward, speeding past Youichiro and snarling like an attack dog.

"Where is she, you bast—"

The last syllable never left his lips, as the man caught him in a textbook perfect *o-soto-gari*. That classic hip throw was one of the first techniques taught in judo, but the broad-shouldered man didn't execute it like a beginner. Kenta glimpsed the dim stars above him before being slammed face-first onto the gravel, his arm twisted behind his back in a joint lock that would have been illegal in formal competition.

No wonder this old guy was able to capture so many healthy young girls!

"Nosy boy! How did you get in here?"

Kenta could only groan as Sasaki hyperextended his arm. Any more pressure and his shoulder would pop.

"Sasaki, stop that at once!" yelled Youichiro. The pain eased as the butler took his knee out of Kenta's back.

"Master Youichiro, are you with this ruffian?"

"Yes. I said let go!"

Sasaki stepped away, allowing Kenta to stand up. Rubbing his shoulder, Kenta put a few more feet between them.

"Sasaki, did you lie to me?" Youichiro's voice was very stern.

"What do you mean, sir?"

"What did you do with the kidnapped girls? While I was visiting my father, what were you doing? What did you do to Karin?"

"I gave the girls their money and sent them home," Sasaki replied crisply. His expression never altered in the slightest. "This evening I was out overseeing an inspection of the Juumonji Group's holdings in Sakurauchi. Karin

would be the high school girl you mentioned yesterday—
has something happened with her?

Youichiro glared at his servant. "In Sakurauchi, you
say? Then you don't mind if we check the mileage on your
car!"

Sasaki's eyes widened slightly. "The car?" Then the
calm mask returned. "Of course not, Master Youichiro. Be
my guest."

Kenta doubted that Youichiro would remember what
the mileage had been, but that brief ripple in Sasaki's facade
was all he needed.

"Dammit, Sasaki! I trusted you!" snapped Youichiro.
Kenta empathized with the note of pained betrayal in his
voice, but they were wasting time here.

Sasaki opened his mouth, but another sound cut him
off. It came from the warehouse behind him—a deep, loud
bellow of shock and surprise.

"Karin!" Kenta began to run, leaving Youichiro to deal
with Sasaki.

The trees had disguised just how close the building
was. Light leaked through shuttered windows—somebody
was definitely inside.

"Karin, are you there?"

Reaching the door, he flung it open. The coppery
smell of blood filled his nostrils. Kenta could only stop and
stare, open-mouthed, at what he saw within.

There was Karin, tied to an old bed frame, a squat,
frog-faced, middle-aged man sitting astride her. And then
there was the blood—so much blood—gallons of it. It was
all over the mattress, the man's shirt, his startled face . . .

and it was still coming out of her—a fountain of it, gushing from her nose.

Kenta's shock was followed by relief. If he'd just seen the blood on the bed and on the man, if it wasn't actually still coming out of her, he would have thought something far, far worse. But as grotesque and inexplicable as this was, he'd seen this before.

The man's face was as red as a demon mask from a *kabuki* play. He choked and sputtered and clawed at his sticky eyes. Losing his balance, he slid off his slippery victim and the soaked mattress beneath, right onto the floor.

Youichiro caught up with him and stopped at his side. Paralyzed by what he saw, he stood there, his eyes widening.

The spray from Karin's nose was a trickle now, a drip, and then just a few red bubbles at her nostrils as she breathed. On the soaked floor, her attacker groaned and sat up, clawing feebly at his face. "What?" he said in a thick voice, spitting her blood out of his mouth. "What happened?"

Kenta's wits were pretty much recovered now; unlike Youichiro, he'd seen such a blood explosion before. It hadn't been as extreme as this, but even that one had produced more of the sticky red spread spray than she should have been able to lose without dying. Yet she hadn't died that time; she'd been fine in less than hour. *Please*, he thought, *please let her be okay now, too.*

The big man groggily made it to his feet, obscuring Karin from view. Kenta jumped into the room and stiff-armed him aside. "Out of the way, you dirty bastard!"

The impact spun the man around and his feet shot out from under him, sending him face-first onto the slippery concrete.

Paying him no attention, Kenta splashed through the pool of blood and jumped onto the bed, gently shaking Karin.

"Kenta? You . . . came. I thought . . . about . . . you."

"Are you hurt? Do you need an ambulance?"

He wiped her face with his shirt. Her cheeks were flushed. "No. I'm okay. Just so, so ashamed . . . all my blood everywhere."

He remembered what a big deal it had been the last time she'd gotten a nosebleed. Even now, having been through all this, she was more embarrassed than anything else.

There were no apparent injuries. She was still fully clothed. They'd been in time. Breathing a big sigh of relief, Kenta tried to undo the ropes that bound her hands.

There was a shout from behind him. "Who gave you permission to come in here, boy? How dare you assault me?!"

Kenta turned, but before he could say anything, Youichiro strode into the room and faced the big, bloodstained man, his handsome face white with fury. "Shut up, you bastard! How dare you do something like this in my house!"

The man looked genuinely shocked. "Youichiro, how can you talk to me like that? I'm your uncle!"

Youichiro raised his hand, causing the big man to recoil. "Yes, Tsuneo, and that unfortunate fact makes me want to vomit, you vile pig." Turning back to Kenta and Karin, he pulled out a cell phone. "We really should call an ambulance. And the police."

Karin raised her head off the bed, her hair sticking to the mattress. "No, I'm fine. Please don't call anybody."

"She has a medical condition in which her body makes too much blood," explained Kenta, again working at her bonds. "Sometimes it builds up and bursts out like this. She'll be weak for a little while, but she's fine."

At least, he hoped she'd be fine. There was so much he didn't know, both about what had really happened here and about her.

Youichiro nodded. He made no move to put his cell phone away. "Then I'll call the police."

"Th-there's no need to do that!" sputtered Tsuneo.

Youichiro stared at him coldly. "Yes, I've figured it out. Sasaki betrayed me to work for you. That's why he suggested the kidnappings. I didn't believe Sasaki would harm the girls, but of course you could. Thought you could get your kicks and satisfy your ambitions at the same time, did you? While my father's in the hospital and my mother's away, you thought you could frame me and take over the Juumonji Group."

He turned back toward the bed and for a moment Kenta saw the anguish in his eyes. Yes, he hated the older man, had hated him all along, but to discover that his own uncle was behind something like this must have been a crushing shock.

"You were scum before you ever threatened Karin, but what you tried to do to her makes you a monster. It's over, Tsuneo." Youichiro opened his phone.

"Wait! Think! If you call the police, you'll only implicate yourself! They'll find out you ordered the kidnappings!"

Youichiro nodded. "I take full responsibility for my part in this. I deserve whatever happens."

"You little punk!" roared Tsuneo, leaping to his feet and hurling himself at his nephew. But he was so slow and clumsy that Youichiro dodged easily, sticking his foot out and tripping him in the process.

"Kenta, get Karin out of here."

Kenta turned his attention from the fight, feeling guilty for forgetting about Karin. *Oh no, she's passed out.* The temporary anemia that followed her blood rushes had set in. Her head lolled to one side, eyes closed. Certain that Youichiro had Tsuneo under control, Kenta resumed working on the ropes around Karin's wrists.

"Do you have some scissors? Or a knife?" he asked, struggling with the tight ropes.

A gasp and then a thud rang out behind him. Looking over his shoulder, Kenta saw Sasaki with his right arm clamped tightly around Youichiro's throat, his left hand bracing the back of the boy's head in what's known as a rear-naked choke.

Staring impassively at Kenta, Sasaki let his former master sprawl limply to the floor.

"Youichiro!" shouted Kenta. "Youichiro, get up!" Youichiro didn't stir. He was completely unconscious.

Expressionless, Sasaki shook his head ever so slightly. He had taken off his shoes so he could sneak up on Youichiro from behind.

"It's regrettable," he said to nobody in particular, "but once things reached this stage, I had no choice. I've said that Master Youichiro was too naive. Look at him, turning his back on me after he knew that I'd betrayed him."

Kenta scrambled off the bed, but he knew that his chances against Sasaki were nil. Despite the vast difference in their ages, he'd end up just like Youichiro.

Still sitting on the floor, Tsuneo cackled with glee. "Nicely done, Sasaki. You've just earned a twenty-five percent bonus." Wheezing, he struggled to his feet. "Give me a hand here."

"I think not, sir," said Sasaki in the same terrifyingly calm tone. "You'll have to manage by yourself. I'll take care of this young man, but what happens to the girl and to Master Youichiro will be on your hands. And you'll give me more than a bonus; you'll double the original offer."

"What?! How dare you try to dicker with me now? You're facing just as much trouble as I am."

Sasaki's blank expression never changed. "Those are my terms. If you don't like them, I shall leave and you can clean up this mess by yourself."

Tsuneo looked at Kenta, who, despite being much thinner, was taller and faster and in much better shape. He looked down at Youichiro, making the obvious mental calculation. The latter might regain consciousness at any moment. It was unlikely that Tsuneo could take Kenta by himself; he wouldn't stand a chance against the two of them, despite his slovenly bulk. He was exhausted already.

"Okay, okay," he wheezed. "I'll do as you say. Just take that boy out. And make sure it hurts."

Sasaki nodded, cracking his knuckles.

Kenta knew he should have been searching for a weapon, but the only reason that Sasaki hadn't rushed him was that he hadn't made a move yet. "You can't really mean to kill Karin and me!"

"No," said Sasaki, "just you. Master Youichiro and the girl are his responsibility. That's what we just negotiated. I would say that I hope you pay better attention than that in school, but your past mistakes don't matter now, since you're not going to be taking any more exams."

Watching Sasaki approach, pokerfaced, Kenta was still paralyzed. This couldn't be happening. Nothing to his right or left looked light enough to pick up and use as a weapon. Behind him there was nothing but small ventilation windows. Even if he could somehow slip past Sasaki, he could hardly run away and leave Karin lying there unconscious.

Dammit, there has to be something! He grit his teeth in anguish.

And then two figures—one large, one small—appeared in the doorway behind Sasaki and Tsuneo.

Kenta blinked. They'd dropped in as if from above. *But how . . . ?*

Before he could ponder the mystery further, a cloud of black, fluttering shapes swarmed in the doorway. Kenta recoiled, but rather than filling the room, they flapped around the two men like a whirlwind of veined, black leaves. They were bigger than moths and didn't fly like birds.

Bats. They were bats. Hundreds of bats.

Screamingly incoherently, Tsuneo and Sasaki swatted at the cloud of flying mammals, but in vain. Dodging not only Tsuneo's slow, meaty hands, but Sasaki's considerably faster ones, the bats settled on their faces. Kenta couldn't believe what he was seeing.

The two men jerked and hopped around for a moment, their heads completely hidden by fluttering black hoods. Then they stiffened and fell like marionettes with their strings cut.

Kenta didn't see what happened next. Another cluster of bats flew straight at him. Dark wings blocked his vision. He felt wind on his face, but no pain. *They aren't biting me, so what . . . ?*

He never completed that thought. Like Tsuneo and Sasaki before him, he slumped, unconscious, onto the floor.

Nobody was awake to see the bats rise into the air in a black column, streaming out the door with the precision of tiny warplanes doing formation maneuvers.

Two figures stepped into the warehouse. One was a tall, striking woman in an elegant burgundy cocktail dress; the other was an angelic-looking little girl in a black satin dress. Calera and Anju.

Several bats still fluttered around them to receive final orders.

"Karin overflowed again," said Anju, holding her pert nose. Even if she'd been old enough to drink human blood, she would hardly have enjoyed smelling that of her own sister.

Calera walked to the bed, moving so elegantly that she seemed to float. She deftly undid Karin's bonds with one sharp fingernail. "Are you all right?" she asked, gently shaking her daughter.

Karin's eyes flickered open. She blinked several times, her lids wet with tears. "Oh, Mama."

"Looks like we were in time. Nobody's hurt you, have they?"

Karin clung to Calera. "It was so scary. And so embarrassing. He was . . . he was going to . . ."

"Shush," soothed Calera, hugging her daughter for all the world like this was a natural thing for her, even though she'd never been the most touchy-feely parent. "You do get yourself into trouble, don't you? So much trouble!" Her words didn't hide the tone of relief in her voice.

Karin suddenly looked around her. "Wait a second, what happened to Kenta? He came to save me!"

"He's asleep," said Anju tersely. A small cluster of bats, which had been clinging to the frame of the door, divided into four parts, settling on the heads of each prone person in the room. "Should I just make them forget Karin was here?" Anju asked her mother.

"Yes, but be extra careful with that rich boy, since he's already broken the spell once." She stroked Karin's head. "Now, now, dear, don't go wrinkling this dress."

Gently shoving Karin away from her, she strode over to Tsuneo. "You smell like a liar. Since you forced me to come all this way here, you shall be my dinner."

Long sharp fangs slid out from beneath her scarlet lips. Pulling Tsuneo up by his shirtfront with inhuman ease, she looked down at his exposed neck. "I do so hate it when they've not had the decency to shave, but vampires can't be choosers." She bit into his fleshy neck, but let go almost immediately.

"Ugh, much too sweet. Never thinks of the consequences, just lies to make himself look important. Such a coarse, unsubtle flavor, and the blood sugar and cholesterol are much too high."

Despite her apparent disdain, she dipped her head like a swan and drank deeply. Finishing, she dropped him with a thud, and then delicately patted her lips with a handkerchief.

"I do hope the other one tastes better."

Calera walked past Kenta without so much as a glance and hoisted Sasaki as easily as she had his master. This time she didn't pause to comment, but drank without interruption.

A minute later, she blotted her lips again. "Ah, yes, much more satisfactory. The lies were well-aged, subtle, and complex. I could drink men like him every day."

When she dropped him, his head bounced like a coconut on the concrete floor, but she paid no notice. "We must leave this place," she said to her children. "Quickly, before someone else comes."

Karin looked at her mother anxiously. "But Mama, is it safe to leave Kenta and Youichiro just lying here like this?"

"Of course it is," said Anju. "That's why Mama drank from those two men. They're not dead, but they won't be a threat anymore. However, if we don't leave soon, I'll have to erase their memories again." She smiled more gently at her sister than she ever had before, and after a moment, Karin nodded her assent.

A few minutes after the three of them left, Youichiro's phone began to ring. Kenta opened his eyes, sat up, and looked around him.

What—what happened here?" There was something dark, wet, and sticky all over the floor, and on his shirt, too. "What is this? Blood? I don't seem to be hurt . . ."

While Kenta was staring around him, the phone continued to ring.

Lying on his face, Youichiro gave a low moan. Rolling over, he pushed himself up with one elbow and fumbled for the phone. Watching him do this, Kenta continued to wrack his brain. *What happened here?*

He could remember coming here looking for Karin. Sasaki had thrown him to the ground, but Youichiro had stopped him. Then they'd heard a man scream and ran into the warehouse. But what happened after that?

Youichiro's uncle and Sasaki were lying on the floor. Both were limp and pale, but breathing, albeit shallowly. Neither looked like they'd wake up anytime soon.

"Yes," said Youichiro hoarsely into the phone. "What? What did you say?" He scrambled to his feet, fully alert now despite the bruise on his throat from Sasaki's forearm. "I'm in the warehouse—I can be back inside in five minutes.

No, I don't know why I'm in the warehouse—that's a good question, but it's not important now. Please, don't let her hang up!"

He snapped the phone shut. "I have to go back to the main house," he said to Kenta.

"What is it?"

Youichiro spun around, his normally impassive face awash in surprise and excitement. "My mother just called. We haven't been able to get in touch with her for months. That's why I've got to get back. What did we come out here for, anyway?"

"You don't remember?"

"I remember coming out here to look for Karin. And something about how these two teamed up to frame me for sexual assault . . ."

"Yeah, I remember that too. But Karin was . . . here? Not here?"

They looked at each other. Something didn't fit. They could remember Sasaki strangling Youichiro, and they could remember Tsuneo sprawled on the ground, but they couldn't remember if Karin had been there or not . . . or what they had done . . . why there was so much blood . . .

Youichiro shook his head. "Anyway, let's go back to the mansion. I want to take this call, and you're a real mess."

"I'm not hurt or anything, but what's with all this blood? And what should we do about *them?*"

"Forget about them for the moment. I don't know what happened, but they don't look like they're going anywhere soon." Back at the mansion, Youichiro took the call from his mother while Kenta borrowed the shower and a change of clothes. Looking at his stained garments in the laundry hamper, his mind reeled.

What in God's name happened out there? He should be worried sick about Karin, but it was as if he somehow knew she was okay. But that didn't make sense. None of it made sense.

The more he thought about it, the less sense it made.

Now in a fresh set of clothing, he returned to the parlor he'd first sat in, but Youichiro was apparently still speaking with his mother long-distance on the house's landline. He showed no signs of returning anytime soon. It seemed rude to just go home. Kenta sprawled on the very comfortable couch and tried to remember what had happened.

We couldn't have been in there more than five minutes. Where did the blood come from? How did Sasaki and Youichiro's uncle get knocked unconscious?

There was a knock and the door opened. But it wasn't Youichiro; it was the housekeeper with some tea and snacks. "Enjoy."

"Thank you. Where's Youichiro?"

"The young master is still on the phone, I'm afraid. Please wait a little longer." Her tone was more polite this time, but not exactly warm. Not surprising, considering the state he'd been in, tracking blood across carpets more expensive than everything in his entire apartment combined. When they had come back to the mansion, Youichiro had prevented her from calling the police. No wonder she was suspicious. Kenta would have been too, if he'd been in her shoes.

A sudden thought struck him. He remembered Youichiro calling Karin earlier, and her not being home, but what about now? She wasn't here, and she had to be *someplace*.

He left the room, found the housekeeper, and asked if he could borrow a phone. Youichiro was still talking with his mother, but an estate like this obviously had more than one outside line.

"Dial zero, then the number, same as you would when calling outside the city," she said, explaining how to use the antique rotary phone that Youichiro had used earlier.

Kenta remembered the number that Youichiro had said belonged to the Maaka residence. He'd made a mental note of it at the time, irked that Youichiro knew it and he didn't.

There'd been so much blood. The only time he'd seen so much blood before was at school, when Karin had her strange attack of what she called "reverse anemia." Could something like that have happened here?

After several rings, a deep male voice came on the line. Her father, presumably.

"Hello?"

"Good evening, sir. My name's Kenta Usui, from the same class as Karin at Shiihaba High School." The receiver shook in his trembling hand. "Is Karin there?"

He expected a long, oppressive silence, but the answer was immediate, and surprisingly cheery. "Why yes, my daughter got back an hour ago, said she was tired, and went to bed early."

"An hour ago?"

That couldn't be right. Kenta glanced at the clock. It didn't match up. While they'd been in the warehouse, Karin couldn't have been at home.

The relaxed voice continued: "If it's important, I could wake her up. But she's quite the sleepyhead, so it may take a while."

"Oh, no, it's just . . . was there anything, you know, unusual about her?"

"Unusual? About my daughter?" The man sounded amused. "Like what?"

"Nothing. Sorry to disturb you."

Kenta hung up. He flopped back down on the sofa, feeling like a huge weight had been taken off his shoulders. *So maybe it wasn't Karin's nosebleed. At least she's safe—that's what matters. None of this makes sense, but at least I know she's safe.*

The snacks were delicious. The tea was warm and soothing. Kenta sighed again.

Whatever happened, she'd gotten home safely. He wished he knew what transpired after she was pulled into that car, but he could ask her about that at school tomorrow, assuming she was willing to talk. The girl was so weird about stuff . . .

Someone knocked at the door twice. It was Youichiro. "Sorry to keep you waiting."

"What's going on with your mother? You're finished talking to her?"

Youichiro shook his head. He remained standing. "Not yet. It looks like it's going to be a long conversation, so I told her I'd call her back and took a break. I didn't want to keep you waiting out here all night still not knowing what happened to Karin."

Kenta pointed at the phone. "I called her house. Her father says she got home okay, and that's she's fine, but sleeping now." He didn't mention the time discrepancy. Youichiro had enough on his mind as it was.

Youichiro's next words were an almost perfect echo of Kenta's earlier thoughts. "I don't know what happened, but I'm glad she's safe."

"Amen to that." Suddenly Kenta felt very tired, but it wasn't a bad kind of fatigue. Despite all the unanswered questions, he felt like he'd accomplished *something*, even if he was unsure what or how.

Youichiro must have seen the weariness on his face. "I don't mean to throw you out, but you should go home and get some rest. I'll get a car to drive you."

Kenta nodded. His mother was probably worried. But there were still those damned hazy memories, as well as two rather large loose ends. "It might be none of my business, but what are you going to do with your butler and your uncle?"

Youichiro shook his head, looking very puzzled. "It's the strangest thing. They came back inside a while ago, but they're acting very odd."

"Trying to pretend nothing happened?" Kenta remembered how smoothly Sasaki had lied outside the warehouse. If Youichiro had not heard Kenta's story, he would have been fooled quite easily.

But Youichiro shook his head. "No, nothing like that. I don't understand it myself, really. We'll talk about it tomorrow at school. By now your parents are probably worried about you."

"There's just my mom, but yeah, she probably is." What to do about Tsuneo and Sasaki was a Juumonji family problem, maybe even a Juumonji Group problem. It was probably difficult for Youichiro to deal with everything while Kenta was in the house.

Youichiro took him as far as the gate, even opening the door so Kenta could climb into the back seat of the Benz.

"Tomorrow at school, then?"

"Yeah. Sorry about today. Good night."

Watching the bright lights speed by outside the window, Kenta tried to figure out how he'd broach the subject with Karin the next day. He never noticed the bat flapping overhead.

The wet, gray skies of previous mornings had given way to a bright one, that was the clear blue color of cornflowers. Bathed in fresh sunlight, the school's ivory walls looked clean and new.

"Hi, Karin," said Fukumi brightly.

"Hello, Fukumi! You're early today," Karin replied, sounding sleepy but also refreshed, somehow.

"Morning practice. See you in class."

Karin walked on toward the building, trying to sort out the events of the previous night. *Anju's bats said everything's taken care of, with Kenta and Youichiro both safe and sound. Still, I can't help worrying.*

Inside the building, hurried footsteps echoed behind her in the hallway. Understandably a bit jumpy, she spun around.

"Karin!" It was Kenta Usui, his typical frown softening into something like relief.

"Um, hi." It was a little easier to look straight into those piercing eyes, but not much. How was she going to answer his questions about the previous night?

"Good morning, Karin." He stepped uncomfortably close, keeping one eye on the students walking past, and lowered his voice. "So, um, last night . . . I know I saw you being grabbed off the street and thrown into the back of a car. Well, I think I did—it's all so weird."

She looked down at her feet. "I know, but I'm okay. What's important is that somebody saved me. I don't remember much after that—next thing I knew, I was at home."

Her parents and Anju had suggested she take this tack and claim to remember as little as the boys did, but she was never comfortable lying, and even less so now, considering what Kenta had done for her.

"You too?" whispered Kenta, dark brows knitting in puzzlement and what might be disappointment. No doubt he'd been hoping she could clear up the mystery.

From the top of the stairs, a voice called out to them. "Hey, Karin! And Kenta! Good, just who I was looking for!" There was Youichiro Juumonji waving over the guardrail, his face more open and animated than she'd seen it before. Smiling, he came bounding down the stairs toward them.

"I was about to swing by your classroom—I've got news about that mess yesterday."

Passersby were staring at them with interest. Kenta scratched his cheek. "How about the roof?" Up there, they'd be away from the crowd and nobody could eavesdrop around a corner.

Despite the blustery wind that blew their hair around, they stood as far from the stairs as possible.

Youichiro looked out over the street, then turned toward Karin and Kenta. "First, I'd like to apologize for getting you two mixed up in this."

Karin started to protest that it hadn't been his fault, but bit her tongue. She wasn't supposed to remember any of that.

Kenta spoke for her. "Your uncle and butler were the bad guys, not you."

"But I can't shirk responsibility. I was too stupid to realize they might be working together and fell right into their trap. I can't remember what happened in the warehouse yesterday, but, Karin . . . were you . . . well . . . hurt in any way?"

Meeting his concerned gaze, Karin shook her head firmly. "No, I was rescued before anything could happen, I do know that much for sure. Maybe not much else, but I do know that. Next thing I recall, I was outside my house, feeling glad it was all over."

Youichiro nodded in relief. "My uncle . . . the thought of what he wanted to do . . . I'm so ashamed. But that's not nearly as important as the fact that you're all right. Still, I'm very sorry."

Kenta butted in. "What happened after I changed and went home? I mean, what did you do with those scumbags?"

Youichiro frowned again. "You may not believe this," he said in a tone that suggested he didn't quite do so himself, "but my uncle and Sasaki seem like different men. It's as if something scared them honest, or as if they had some sort of life-altering experience, like surviving a plane crash. They confessed to everything, in the greatest detail, without the slightest amount of coercion—all their plans, everything they'd done. I expected them to at least try to pin all the blame on each other, but no, it was nothing like that. My uncle admitted to molesting those poor girls. Sasaki admitted that he'd known about it all along and was a willing accomplice. They both say they're ready to go to prison. It's weird."

Kenta's frown deepened in disbelief, but Karin merely nodded. Of course, she knew what had happened. Her mother had sucked the liar's blood right out of them. That's why Anju had said they wouldn't be a threat anymore—not just because they were too weak to move for a while, but because they'd been permanently changed.

Youichiro continued speaking in a soft voice. "I intended to call the police, but after consulting with my mother, we've decided to leave matters up to the kidnapped victims."

"I hope they press charges," said Kenta. "Those bastards should rot in prison. But at least the kidnappings have stopped." He looked at Karin, then quickly looked away. "And Karin will be safe."

Embarrassed by his embarrassment, Karin searched for an opportunity to change the subject. "So you got in touch with your mother?" she asked Youichiro.

Youichiro's frown morphed into a beaming smile. "Yes! All this time I couldn't contact her, I assumed it was because she hated my father and she wanted nothing to do with him or with me. But it wasn't that at all."

Youichiro's mother had been in a convent in Germany for two months, reevaluating her own feelings in solitude and quiet. With no access to television, newspapers or the Internet, she'd had no idea what was happening to her own family or anything else in the world. When at last she decided that the marriage was worth saving, she left the convent, only to discover that her husband had been in an accident and was now in a coma.

The shock had galvanized her into action. Where most wives would have been forced to content themselves with rushing to their husbands' bedsides and playing a fruitless waiting game, she'd immediately put all her wealth and social contacts to the best possible use. Discovering that a clinic in Switzerland was gaining renown for its revolutionary approach to coma patient care and rehabilitation, she'd procured him the first available bed there.

"They're going to be able to fly your father to Switzerland?"

"Yes. They say it won't harm him to fly. And I'm going to accompany him."

"You are?" said Kenta, unable to hide his surprise. This was the boy who couldn't bring himself to visit his father's hospital bed, after all.

Youichiro bowed his head. "Yes. I thought long and hard about what you said last night. I can't keep running away." He looked up and ran one hand through his windblown hair. "Oh, it's not finalized yet. I need to talk to all the kidnapping victims, to see if they'll accept my apology and if there's anything else I can do for them. I don't know how long I'll have to talk to the police, either. But however long that takes, once it's over, I'll go to Switzerland. My mother is going to be far too busy running the Juumonji Group, so it's up to me to look after my father. I'll sit by him and talk to him every day. My mother will visit as much as she can."

"Oh, good!" said Karin. "It sounds like there's a lot more hope that way."

"Wait," said Kenta, not quite following all this. "If you go to Switzerland, you'll have to quit school, right? So after all you've put Karin through, you're just going to drop her and head overseas?"

Youichiro looked away from both of them. "Well, um, I wouldn't put it like that . . ."

"Stop!" said Karin. She had something she needed to say before Youichiro opened his mouth. Bowing apologetically, she shouted, in one breath, "I'm so sorry—I really am—but I really, *really* can't go out with you, Youichiro!"

Both boys responded simultaneously.

"What?"

"Really?"

Crap, I shouldn't have said that with Kenta right here! Karin thought.

Her eyes met his. If there was such a thing as a happy glare, that would describe his expression right now.

Or at least so she thought, for he turned his back pretty quickly.

"If we're finished talking about the kidnappings, I've got to get back to class," he said over his shoulder as he headed toward the stairs. His shoulders were slumped in embarrassment, but there was a skip in his step.

"Sorry I got you mixed up in all this!" shouted Youichiro after him. "And thanks for your advice!"

Kenta didn't say anything, but his silent wave seemed to signal both "forget it" and "you're welcome" as his dark hair bobbed out of sight down the stairwell.

Sighing, Karin turned back to Youichiro. "I'm really sorry."

She hadn't been asleep when Kenta had called her house the previous night, but instead had been lying in bed, thinking everything over. When she'd been in gravest danger, it was Kenta's face she'd thought of, not this boy's. If she couldn't think of Youichiro Juumonji when facing her own death, then they had no future together.

Youichiro looked at Karin and nodded, his frown becoming a bittersweet smile. "No, I'm the one who should apologize to you."

"To me?"

"Yes. Kenta's advice—well, his scolding, really—made me think some things over. He accused me of running away from reality. And he was right. If I hadn't done that, Sasaki and my uncle would never have been able to move against me."

Karin didn't understand. "That was their fault, not yours."

He put his hands on his head and arched his back, looking up at the sky, his face like porcelain in the clear morning light. "Like I said before, I'm not off the hook that easily. After I spoke with my mother yesterday, I thought things over some more. The most important thing for me right now is to get my father well and put my family back together. At a time like this I have no right to go asking anyone out. I could never put a girl first, not even a girl who deserves that as much as you do. So I must withdraw the yesterday's offer."

He craned his head to the side and flashed her an awkward grin. "Except I guess I don't need to, since you've already done me the kindness of turning it town."

There was no irony or bitterness in the way he'd said that.

"Not that being rejected makes me want to jump for joy. All my life there have been people who smiled politely and gave me compliments—one eye on the Juumonji name and the Juumonji Group. But you and Kenta were different."

He said he felt sad, but there was no confusion or hesitation in his voice, only pleasure. "My father hasn't recovered yet, and maybe he never will. But there's new hope… and a new me. I know what I need to do. And whatever happens, my mother doesn't really want a divorce. So maybe you're my goddess of Fortune after all, Karin Maaka."

"Oh, I'm nothing like that!" mumbled Karin, shaking her head and blushing.

She hadn't bitten him again; she'd never injected her own blood into him. Youichiro hadn't become lucky, but he'd achieved something else. Contentment. And that was something he'd done entirely by himself.

"Tomorrow or the next day, I'm going to withdraw from this school," he continued, pretending to look at the same patch of sky as she was. "Then, even if I do go to Switzerland, would you mind if I called you, or e-mailed? As a friend, I mean. I want to ask Kenta the same thing."

Karin started to nod, then caught herself. "Wait a minute, Youichiro—you don't need Kenta's permission to be friends with me! I mean, it's not like we're together or anything!" Her face was warm with more than just sunlight.

Youichiro stiffened. "No, no, I meant that I think he's a good guy and I want to stay in touch with him, too, that's all."

Karin realized her mistake. "Oh. Yes, of course! Forget I said that."

Youichiro relaxed and laughed gently. "But I do see why you turned me down now. You've chosen Kenta. You guys should be good for each other." There was no sarcasm in his words.

"No, really, it's nothing like that!"

Youichiro turned toward her, forcing her to meet his eyes. "Really?"

It was really hot on the roof. *If it feels like this right now, what's the rest of the day going to be like?* But of course that heat was really coming from inside Karin.

Taking her silence as his answer, Youichiro nodded, and then suddenly reached down and took her hand in his.

Karin's mouth formed an *O* of surprise, but before she could protest, he leaned over and pressed his lips to the back of her hand.

Yikes! Were her knees knocking together?

He smiled at her, not so wistfully now, but content. "Thank you, Lady Luck. Goodbye. Take care of Kenta." Not waiting for her response, he turned and walked away.

Karin was left alone on the roof, staring vacantly into the distance. *Take care of Kenta? But there's really nothing between us!*

He was just a classmate, just a coworker, that was all. Well, that should have been all. But when she thought about him, she could feel her face glow like the sun. Karin put her hands on her cheeks, waiting for the drumming in her chest to subside. After a while, the wind on the roof began to cool her off.

At last she heard the warning bell ring.

And so another day begins. So much to think about.

She ran down the stairs, if not gracefully, at least with a lighter step than usual.

At lunch, as always, Karin and Maki ate together. Through the open window, they could hear cicadas singing in the noonday heat.

"Today would be a great day for gym class to be in the pool," said Maki wistfully. Karin looked out the window at an airplane leaving a white trail across the sky. She closed her empty lunchbox.

What are the odds of that being Youichiro's plane? Pretty low, I guess.

For a while she let her mind trace shapes in the tumbled clouds the airplane passed. It was five days since the kidnapping. Youichiro had apologized to all of the victims. They'd seemed to understand, apparently not wanting to punish his uncle at the cost of disgracing him. The police didn't need him.

Three days before, he had withdrawn from Shiihaba High School. Before that, because his theatrical courtship of Karin had been replaced by a comfortable friendship, rumors spread that he'd dumped her, and the girls who'd once disdained or even threatened Karin now treated her with sympathy and even friendship. Though they did have a tendency to pump her for details about him.

But that was yesterday's news once Youichiro left the school. Exam results were posted and conversation turned to makeup tests and summer holidays. With the rich boy who'd only attended for a few days now gone, the school went back to the way it had always been. There'd be new scandals and sensations. Karin was probably the only one thinking about the fact that Youichiro was leaving the country today—something he'd told her about in an e-mail the previous night.

Watching Karin watch the plane, Maki said, "So, are you studying for makeup tests?"

"I should be." Remembering that she had failed almost all her subjects, Karin felt depressed. This was no time for gazing at the sky.

Maki made a sympathetic face. "I barely scraped by, myself. Which means I can't help you study."

Karin's eyes widdened. She'd been counting on Maki's help. "Why not?"

Maki sighed. "Sure, I'd like to, but though I don't have any makeup tests, they gave me lots of extra practice."

Karin's fingers drummed nervously on her lunchbox. "Oh, I understand. But yikes . . . what am I gonna do? Everyone will be busy with practice."

Maki shrugged, then smiled wickedly. "Guess you'll just have to ask Kenta."

Karin stuck her tongue out at her friend. "Why is it always Kenta, Kenta, Kenta? I keep telling you, he's just another boy; someone I work with and have class with!" She was trying to hide her embarrassment with mock anger, but she could feel her cheeks getting warm.

Even Youichiro thought I was carrying a torch for Kenta. But I'm not! I'm so not!

Maki might have pretended not to notice how much she was blushing, but it was unlikely that anyone else around her would be so kind. She had to get out of here before her physical reaction drew hoots and jeers.

She stood up. "I'm on duty today, so I better go help set up for chemistry—I'll see you later."

That last was spoken over her shoulder as she rushed to the door. But of course she slammed into someone on the way out. "Oops, sorry!"

"Hey, watch where you're going! Oh—hi Karin."

Looking up, she saw spiky chestnut hair and not-really-sinister eyes.

Oh no, why does this always happen to me?

Her body temperature rose. Sweat ran down her face, neck, and legs. Her heart kick-started like a motorcycle.

Nooooo!

Hands clapped over her mouth to stifle her own cry of anguish, she bolted past him, out into the hall.

Flustered, Kenta shouted after her. "Hey, watch out! The janitor spilled some oil on the floor out there!"

Before her brain could process his warning, her shoes slipped out from under her and she slid down the hall on her butt. Right toward the wall.

Back in the room she'd just left, Maki winced at the sound of someone crashing into a row of lockers. The impact echoed down the hallway.

Outside the window, the cicadas in the trees all flew upward in a panic, scrambling toward the thinning vapor trail of the departing plane.

Greetings. I am Tohru Kai. Thank you for reading.

This book is a novelization of Yuna Kagesaki's hit manga *Karin*, currently running in the magazine Monthly Dragon Edge. But it's a side story rather than a direct adaptation of the manga storyline. So while you can of course enjoy the novel its own, it will be twice as much fun if you read it along with the manga. [Called *Chibi Vampire* in English.]

For those of you who are collecting the manga, this book takes place in the few days between the magazine issues five and six. So while you're waiting for the second volume of the manga to be released, you can enjoy this novel. Perfect timing, eh?

In order to write this novel, the first thing I did was read the *Karin* manga. If I didn't know anything about her, how on earth could I write it?

Reading it, this is what I thought:

Wow. She's cute. She's really insanely cute, that Karin Maaka!

Dragon Edge's blurb calls *Karin* "an embarrassing school love comedy."

Embarrassing. Anyone who felt that word pierce them right in the heart, raise your hands.

You almost never see embarrassed girls these days. We're an endangered species. Maybe we need a governmental preservation plan.

The other day I heard someone talking about the following on television. On a train station platform, a group of high school girls on a class trip were waiting. Naturally, they were all in uniform, and several of them sat cross-legged in very short skirts. But when anyone looked appalled at their behavior, rather than looking away, they glared back and shouted: "eyes to yourself, you dirty pervert!"

So wrong, girls, so very wrong!

As someone who very much likes cute girls, I wanted to object loudly. Sure, it's fine to pay attention to your makeup and the way you dress. But if only the exterior needed to be cute, then everyone would just look at pictures.

But flesh and blood girls are cute because of their attitude and body language. Nobody will be happy if you flash your panties around casually! A rare flower has value precisely because it almost never shows its bloom. When the wind blows your skirt up and you hurriedly push it back down, blushing a deep red—now that sight is the true meaning of cute!

Excuse me; I seem to have drifted off topic. I was talking about embarrassment.

Even now, Karin is embarrassed.

Certainly, in the manga, there is a scene where she falls down and shows her panties, but a moment later she hurriedly pulls her skirt back down, shrieking in panic. Not only that, she is also hideously embarrassed by her un-vampire-like condition, which makes her cheeks turn red—and after Kenta carries her home and she's alone in bed, she says, "I'm too embarrassed to sleep!" and pulls the covers over her head. Pure, unadulterated embarrassment.

So cuuuuuute.

Having this character placed in my hands is a grave responsibility.

But as I said earlier, I love cute girls. And vampires.

My joy at being allowed to do this book balances out the grave sense of responsibility. I did my best to write a novel that does the original work justice and keeps Karin cute.

If those of you who have finished reading were satisfied, then so am I.

Intelligent readers will have already guessed that this means there are plans afoot for the second volume.

This time the guest character was a high school boy, so next time I think I'll introduce a girl. I like writing boys, but if it's all boys all the time, then it's like my color palette is rather drab.

I very much want there to be girls. Cute girls or beautiful girls. Just thinking about how to get whatever type of girl I decide to create mixed up with the main characters makes me happy.

I hope you also choose to read the second novel.

And if you were wondering what other things this crazy Tohru Kai woman wrote, you can certainly visit my website "The Old School Building" [in Japanese only] at http://www.occn.zaq.ne.jp/kai-tohru/. There you will find information on all the novels I've published and the manga I've scripted.

And finally, to the creator of this series and the illustrator for this novel, Kagesaki Yuna, to my *tantou* Y-san, to all the editors at *Fujimi Mystery Bunko,* and to anyone else who may have played a hand in the publishing of this book, plus to all you readers: Thank you from the bottom of my heart.

—2003, November.

(It rained very hard all morning, completely ignoring the weather report.)

The best of humanity in the worst of wars.

SEIKAI
CREST OF THE STARS ™

THE NEW MANGA NOVEL SERIES FROM TOKYOPOP

SCI-FI